W9-AAZ-057

Targeting the
CTB-TerraNova

Reading and Language Arts • Mathematics

Harcourt Achieve

Rigby • Steck-Vaughn

www.HarcourtAchieve.com

1.800.531.5015

Harcourt Achieve Inc. is indebted to the following for permission to use material in this book:

page 16: "My Korean Name" by Leonard Chang from *Highlights for Children*, August 1999, Vol. 54. Copyright © 1999 by Highlights for Children, Inc., Columbus, Ohio. Reprinted with permission.

page 33: "Pot of Potatoes" from *Growing Things* by Tina and Neil Morris. Copyright © 1994 by Franklin Watts. Used with permission of Franklin Watts, a division of Grolier Publishing Company, 90 Sherman Turnpike, Danbury, CT 06816. All rights reserved. Now a division of Scholastic Library Publishing.

page 42: Reprinted with permission from *A Thousand Pails of Water* by Ronald Roy. Copyright © 1993 by Ronald Roy.

page 48: *I Have a Sister; My Sister Is Deaf* by Jeanne Whitehouse Peterson. Text copyright © 1997 by Jeanne Whitehouse Peterson. Used by permission of HarperCollins Publishers.

page 60: Adapted from *Wagon Wheels* by Barbara Brenner. Copyright © 1978 by Barbara Brenner. Used by permission of HaperCollins Publishers.

Photo Credits:
p. 27 ©Otto Greule/Allsport; p. 37 ©Joe McDonald/Corbis; p. 58 AP/Wide World Photos; p. 63 ©G. Rothstein/NYT Permissions.

The CTB and TerraNova tests are published by CTB McGraw-Hill. Such company has neither endorsed nor authorized this test-preparation book.

ISBN: 0-7398-9752-7

Targeting the
CTB-TerraNova
Grade 4
CONTENTS

Dear Parent or Educator,

Welcome to **Targeting the CTB-TerraNova**. You have selected a book that will help your child develop the skills he or she needs to succeed on the CTB-TerraNova.

Although testing can be a source of anxiety for children, this book will give your child the preparation and practice that he or she needs to feel better prepared and more confident when taking the CTB-TerraNova. Research shows that children who are acquainted with the scoring format of standardized tests score higher on those tests. Students also score higher when they practice and understand the skills and objectives covered on the test.

This book has many features that will help you prepare your child to take the CTB-TerraNova:

- Lessons for the child about how to answer test questions and hints to guide the child toward the correct response
- Test-taking tips
- Tests that simulate the actual CTB-TerraNova tests
- A complete answer key

If your child expresses anxiety about taking a test or completing these lessons, help him or her understand what causes the stress. Then, talk about ways to eliminate anxiety. Above all, enjoy this time you spend with your child. He or she will feel your support, and test scores will improve as success in test taking is experienced.

Help your child maintain a positive attitude about taking a standardized test such as the CTB-TerraNova. Let your child know that each test provides an opportunity to shine.

Sincerely,

The Educators and Staff of
Harcourt School Supply

P.S. You might want to visit our website at www.HarcourtSchoolSupply.com for more test preparation materials as well as additional review of content areas.

Section
A

Reading and Language Arts

About Section A: Reading and Language Arts

This section of the book has been developed to refresh basic skills, familiarize your child with test formats and directions, and teach test-taking strategies. This section of the book is divided into three components: Lessons, Review Tests, and Comprehensive Test.

Lessons

There are lessons on reading comprehension and language arts skills assessed on the CTB-TerraNova Reading and Language Arts test. Each lesson contains:

- *Try This:* a skill strategy that enables your child to approach each lesson in a logical manner
- *Sample:* to familiarize your child with test-taking items
- *Think It Through:* the correct answer to the sample item and an explanation that tells why the correct answer is correct and why the incorrect answers are wrong
- several practice questions based on the lesson and modeled on the kinds of items found on the CTB-TerraNova

Review Test

The lessons are followed by a short Review Test that covers all the skills in the lessons. This test is designed to provide your child with independent practice that will familiarize him or her with the testing situation.

Comprehensive Test

The last component in this section is a Comprehensive Test. This test gives your child an opportunity to take a test under conditions that parallel those he or she will face when taking the CTB-TerraNova Reading and Language Arts test.

In order to simulate the CTB-TerraNova test as closely as possible, we have suggested time limits for the Comprehensive Test. This will enable your child to experience test taking under the same structured conditions that apply when achievement tests are administered. Furthermore, your child will have a final opportunity to apply the skills he or she has learned in this section prior to taking the CTB-TerraNova.

The recommended time limits are:
    Part 1: 40 minutes
    Part 2: 60 minutes

Have your child use the Reading and Language Arts Test Answer Sheet on page 109 to record the answers for this comprehensive test.

Answer Key

The Answer Key at the back of the book contains the answers for all the questions found in this section.

Reading

Directions: Read each story carefully. Then read each question. Darken the circle for the correct answer.

 More than one answer may seem correct. Pick the choice that goes best with the story.

Sample

A Beautiful Cat

The leopard is a beautiful animal. It is the third largest cat. Only the lion and tiger are larger. Leopards are quick and graceful. Most are light tan with black spots close together. There are also black leopards. They have spots too, but the spots are hard to see.

This passage is mainly about

A lions and tigers

B leopards' spots

C cats

D leopards

 The correct answer is <u>D, leopards</u>. This is the best answer. The story includes information about lions and tigers and spots. But that is only part of the story. All the sentences are about leopards.

Answers
S Ⓐ Ⓑ Ⓒ Ⓓ

Directions: Read this passage about an exciting job. Then read each question. Darken the circle for the correct answer.

A World of Secrets

Spying has been around for a long, long time. Especially during wartime there is a lot of spying going on. Each side wants to find out what the other side is doing. We know many famous spies from the American Revolution. Paul Revere was one famous American spy.

The British also had spies during the Revolution. John Howe was a British spy. He found out a lot of information about the Americans. He knocked on the door of an American's house. He told the man living there that he was a spy for the Americans. He said he was hiding from the British. The man trusted him. He told him all about where guns and other weapons were stored. Howe told all this to the British. The United States is lucky that this did not help the British win the war!

When a spy has a message to send, he or she has to make sure that not everyone can read it. Today we have all kinds of computer equipment that can send secret messages. Years ago, however, people used invisible ink. Spies would write their messages with invisible ink. Anyone who saw the message would only see a blank piece of paper. But the person to whom the letter had been sent knew how to uncover the message.

You can pretend to be a spy. Just follow these directions for making your own secret messages.

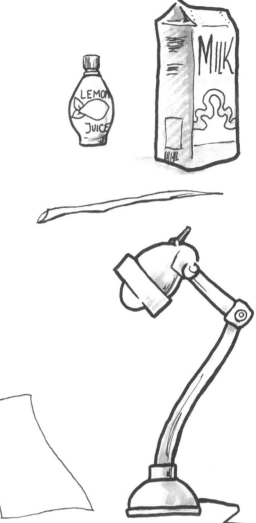

I Put together the things you will need. Get some milk or lemon juice and a small stick with a point. You'll also need a blank piece of paper and a lamp.

2 Dip the stick into the milk or lemon juice. Then use the stick to write your note on the piece of paper. Let the paper dry.

3 To read the message, hold the paper under a lamp that is turned on. Do not let the paper or your hands touch the light bulb! It is hot. Keep the side with the writing near the bulb. Take the paper away from the lamp. The invisible writing will have turned brown. Now you can read the secret message!

1 This passage is mostly about

A spying

B invisible writing

C John Howe

D messages

2 What secret did John Howe tell the British?

F Howe told them he was a spy for the Americans.

G Howe told them where the Americans hid their guns.

H Howe told them how they could win the war.

J Howe told them where the Americans were hiding.

3 Years ago people used <u>invisible</u> ink.

Another word for <u>invisible</u> is

A message
B white
C unseen
D pale

4 The stick that you use in Steps 1 and 2 is like a

F secret weapon
G straw
H tool
J wand

5 What most likely turns the invisible writing brown?

A the paper
B the air
C the light from the lamp
D the heat from the light bulb

6 The last paragraph is mostly about

F how to see the invisible writing
G what is needed to pretend to be a spy
H when to read an invisible message
J where to find a safe place

Answers

3 Ⓐ Ⓑ Ⓒ Ⓓ   5 Ⓐ Ⓑ Ⓒ Ⓓ

10 4 Ⓕ Ⓖ Ⓗ Ⓙ   6 Ⓕ Ⓖ Ⓗ Ⓙ

Directions: Here is a story about a very strange bird, the dodo bird. Read this story carefully. Then read each question. Darken the circle for the correct answer.

The Days of the Dodo

The dodo was a funny looking bird. It stood three feet tall, a little larger than a turkey. It was gray in color and weighed about fifty pounds. A painting of it shows it looking fat and lumpy. Even though the dodo couldn't fly, it had stubby little wings. Each wing had only a few feathers. It had a huge hooked beak, which was as long as nine inches. On top of all that, it had huge yellow feet.

Today there are no more dodos. They are extinct. The last one was killed in 1681. The dodos lived on an island in the Indian Ocean. There were no humans or other animals on the island, so the birds lost their skill of flying. After all, there were no enemies to fly away from. Because of their weight and large feet, they could not run either.

About 500 years ago, some sailors landed on the island. The dodos waddled right up to the sailors. Soon the sailors started using the animals as a source of food. More and more people came to the island. They brought with them dogs, monkeys, pigs, and rats. The dodos had their nests on the ground. The animals ran over the dodos' nests and ate the eggs. The poor dodo birds didn't stand a chance.

Go

7 About how much did the dodos weigh?

A nine pounds

B fifty pounds

C five hundred pounds

D less than a turkey

8 The selection says that dodos are <u>extinct</u>.

That means the birds are

F strong

G not able to fly

H hunted

J no longer living

9 Why do you think the dodos waddled right up to the sailors?

A They wanted to eat the sailors.

B They did not know that the sailors could hurt them.

C They thought the sailors would feed them.

D They wanted to be the sailors' pets.

Answers

7 Ⓐ Ⓑ Ⓒ Ⓓ   **9** Ⓐ Ⓑ Ⓒ Ⓓ

8 Ⓕ Ⓖ Ⓗ Ⓙ

10 Which sentence best explains why the dodo was different from other birds?

  F It was gray.

  G It looked fat and lumpy.

  H It had a nine-inch beak.

  J It could not fly.

11 Which is something the dodo could do?

  A

  B

  C

  D

12 The author wrote, "The poor dodo birds didn't stand a chance."

What does that mean?

  F The dodo birds died because they stood around all day.

  G The dodo birds had no luck.

  H There were too many things against the dodo birds.

  J Everyone feels bad for the dodo birds.

Answers
10 Ⓕ Ⓖ Ⓗ Ⓙ   12 Ⓕ Ⓖ Ⓗ Ⓙ
11 Ⓐ Ⓑ Ⓒ Ⓓ

Directions: Read the story carefully. Then read the question. Darken the circle for the correct answer.

Sample

Household Chores

Cindy often helps her father with the household chores. She sorts the clothes before they are washed. She cleans out the bird's cage. Sometimes she vacuums her room.

What does Cindy do before the clothes are washed?

A   She sorts the clothes.

B   She cleans out the bird's cage.

C   She folds the clothes.

D   She vacuums her room.

Directions: Read these instructions for how to make papier-mâché. Then read each question. Darken the circle for the correct answer.

Making Papier-Mâché

Papier-mâché is easy to make and fun to use. If you use your imagination, you can create just about anything you want using papier-mâché.

1. Gather newspaper, scissors, flour, water, a spoon, and a bowl.

2. Cut or tear the newspaper into strips.

3. Mix a cup of flour and half a cup of water in the bowl until smooth.

4. Dip the newspaper into the flour and water mixture until it is completely wet.

5. Then form the wet newspaper into the shape you want. You can make animals, bowls, jewelry, masks, and many other things in this way.

6. Let the wet papier-mâché dry for several days. It will become very hard.

7. Then you can paint it and decorate it with colored paper, feathers, or buttons if you want.

Answers
S   Ⓐ Ⓑ Ⓒ Ⓓ

1 Which of these is <u>not</u> necessary when making papier-mâché?

   A   letting the papier-mâché objects dry for several days

   B   dipping the newspaper strips into the flour and water mixture

   C   using paint and colored paper to decorate the papier-mâché objects

   D   forming the wet newspaper into a shape

2 How long does it take for the papier-mâché to dry?

   F   a year

   G   two weeks

   H   several days

   J   a few hours

3 Which would <u>not</u> be a good choice for making from papier-mâché?

   A   **C**

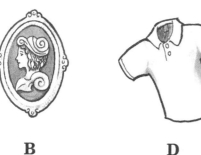

   B   **D**

Answers

1 Ⓐ Ⓑ Ⓒ Ⓓ   **3** Ⓐ Ⓑ Ⓒ Ⓓ

2 Ⓕ Ⓖ Ⓗ Ⓙ

Directions: Here is a story about a boy and his grandfather. Read the story carefully. Then read each question. Darken the circle for the correct answer.

My Korean Name

by Leonard Chang

My grandfather left Korea to live with us in New York when he was almost eighty years old. My parents fixed up the attic so that he had his own room.

He wore traditional Korean clothes: shiny vests with gold buttons, and puffy pants that made his legs look fat even though he was really very skinny. He chewed on small dried fish snacks that smelled up everything. He coughed a lot.

My grandfather spoke only Korean, so I never understood what he was saying. He scared me. I had never seen anyone so old so close.

My mother gave him a goat-hair brush, rice paper, an ink stick, and an inkstone to practice his calligraphy, a special kind of writing.

One day I was watching him draw lines on the paper. He drew some stick figures overlapping each other, swirling his brush easily, quickly. "Won," he said, pointing.

He drew another figure, this time going slowly. The brush made a *swish* sound on the rice paper. He pointed to this second figure and said, "Chul." Bringing me nearer so that I could study the picture, he said, "Won Chul. You."

"That's my name?"

He nodded. "Won Chul."

"That looks neat," I said.

He pushed it toward me.

"For me?" I asked.

"For Won Chul," he said.

My mother later told me that this was *hanja*, a special Korean way of writing using the Chinese alphabet. This was the hanja version of my Korean name. She said, "Your grandfather was once a famous artist. All the people in his town wanted him to draw their names."

"Wow," I said, holding the rice paper carefully.

"You know what your name means, don't you?" she said. "It means 'Wise One.' Do you remember?"

"I remember," I said. I held up my Korean name to the light, the paper so thin it glowed.

4 **This passage mostly tells about**

    F   the grandfather's life in Korea

    G   the author's childhood

    H   what happens between a boy and his grandfather

    J   how to write using calligraphy

5 **What is *hanja*?**

    A   dried fish snacks

    B   traditional Korean clothing

    C   a special kind of Korean writing

    D   a form of rice paper

6 **Which is <u>not</u> something the grandfather used in his calligraphy?**

    F   a goat-hair brush

    G   a ballpoint pen

    H   rice paper

    J   an ink stick

7 **How did the boy feel about his grandfather by the end of the story?**

    A   scared

    B   envious

    C   distrustful

    D   impressed

8 Which sentence from the story supports your answer to question 7?

    F   I had never seen anyone so old so close.

    G   "Wow," I said, holding the rice paper carefully.

    H   One day I was watching him draw lines on the paper.

    J   "You know what your name means, don't you?" she said.

9 He drew some stick figures, <u>swirling</u> his brush easily.

A word that means the ⬚opposite of <u>swirl</u> is

    A   straighten

    B   circle

    C   move

    D   twist

10 What made the rice paper glow?

    F   its thinness

    G   its size

    H   its color

    J   its weight

Answers

8 Ⓕ Ⓖ Ⓗ Ⓙ   10 Ⓕ Ⓖ Ⓗ Ⓙ

9 Ⓐ Ⓑ Ⓒ Ⓓ

Language Arts

Directions: Read each sample. Darken the circle for the correct answer.

Pretend that you are writing this sentence. Choose the word(s) that belongs in the blank. Think of the rules you have learned.

Sample A

Sailors _____ for the slow moving dodo.

A searched

B searches

C searching

D has searched

The correct answer is A, searched. The verb must agree with the subject. "Searches" and "has searched" do not agree with the plural subject. "Searching" is not a verb that can stand on its own.

Choose the sentence that best combines both the sentences into one. Make sure the sentence you choose has the same meaning as the two separate sentences.

Sample B

We bought ice cream cones.

We ate them on the way home.

F Buying the ice cream cones, we ate them on the way.

G After we bought them, we ate them on the way home.

H We bought ice cream cones and ate them on the way home.

J Eating them on the way home, we bought ice cream cones.

The correct answer is H, We bought ice cream cones and ate them on the way home. This is the only choice in which the action is in the correct order.

Answers
SA Ⓐ Ⓑ Ⓒ Ⓓ
20 SB Ⓕ Ⓖ Ⓗ Ⓙ

Directions: Choose the word or words that belong in the blanks. Darken the circle for the correct answer.

The first time the circus will perform will be on ___(1)___.
The first town they will stop in is ___(2)___.

1   **A**   September, 21, 2005

    B   September 21 2005

    C   September 21, 2005

    D   September, 21 2005

2   **F**   Godfrey, Illinois

    G   Godfrey Illinois

    H   godfrey illinois

    J   godfrey, illinois

3   New York City is where _____ was born.

    A   them

    B   us

    C   he

    D   him

4   Of all the players on the team, Grandpa was the _____.

    F   strong

    G   stronger

    H   strongest

    J   most strongest

5   **Choose the sentence that is written correctly.**

    A   A blank sheet of paper.

    B   With the pen near the paper.

    C   You need milk or lemon juice.

    D   Messages hidden in the bottle.

Answers

1   Ⓐ Ⓑ Ⓒ Ⓓ   3   Ⓐ Ⓑ Ⓒ Ⓓ   5   Ⓐ Ⓑ Ⓒ Ⓓ

2   Ⓕ Ⓖ Ⓗ Ⓙ   4   Ⓕ Ⓖ Ⓗ Ⓙ

Lesson 3: Writing Strategies

Directions: Read each sample. Darken the circle for the correct answer.

 Choose the sentence that best completes the story. Try each answer in place of the missing sentence. Only one belongs in the story. Pick the one that makes the most sense in the story.

Sample A

When we came home from vacation, I was so happy. _____. It had been the best trip of my life.

A I did nothing while I was away.

B I had a great time in Virginia.

C I wanted to go back to school.

D I didn't want to go on vacation again.

 The correct answer is <u>B, I had a great time in Virginia</u>. This is the only sentence that makes sense in the story. The other sentences do not complete the story.

 Here is a topic sentence. Pick the sentences that best support it. Try reading each choice after the topic sentence.

Sample B

Here's how to do this magic trick.

F I like to watch magic on television. It seems so real.

G We went to the circus. I saw a magician there.

H Get some dry dirt. We are going to make the dirt disappear.

J He could not believe his eyes. The card had disappeared.

 The correct answer is <u>H, Get some dry dirt. We are going to make the dirt disappear</u>. This is the only sentence that explains the main idea of the story. The other choices are about magic. But they are not about telling you how to do a magic trick.

Answers

SA Ⓐ Ⓑ Ⓒ Ⓓ

SB Ⓕ Ⓖ Ⓗ Ⓙ

Directions: Choose the sentence that best completes the story. Darken the circle for the correct answer.

1 | Put together the things you need to go camping. _____. Remember, there are no stores in the woods!

   A   Only pack what you can carry.

   B   All campers have at least one flashlight.

   C   I always pack my sleeping bag first.

   D   It is very important to be prepared.

2 | _____. She feeds the monkey bananas every day. She makes sure the monkey has enough water to drink.

   F   Ming's cat is a beautiful animal.

   G   Ming's monkey likes to sit on Ming's shoulder.

   H   Ming takes very good care of her monkey.

   J   Ming wants her mother to buy her a monkey.

3   **Which sentences best supports this topic sentence?**

   On rainy days, I like to read.

   A   I play board games when my friends come over. We never care who wins.

   B   I like to read fairy tales more than anything else. They all have happy endings.

   C   I am nine years old. I live in a big old house.

   D   My chair is right next to the window. When I sit in it, I can see what's happening outside.

4   **Choose the sentence that best completes this story about the age of a tree.**

   After a tree is cut down, you can see rings on the stump. _____. The more rings you count, the older the tree is.

   F   The number of rings tells a tree's age.

   G   Tree rings are narrow near the center.

   H   The tree in my yard is very old.

   J   You can use the stump to sit on.

Answers

1 Ⓐ Ⓑ Ⓒ Ⓓ   3 Ⓐ Ⓑ Ⓒ Ⓓ

2 Ⓕ Ⓖ Ⓗ Ⓙ   4 Ⓕ Ⓖ Ⓗ Ⓙ

Lesson 4: Editing Skills

Directions: Read the draft. Then read each sample. Darken the circle for the correct answer.

¹· At the end of the school day, our class presented a play. ²· All the fourth-grade classes came to see it. ³· The play last for over an hour. ⁴· Everyone laughed at the end.

 Choose the best way to rewrite sentence 3. More than one answer may seem correct. But only one answer is correct.

Sample A

A   The play lasts for over an hour.

B   The play lasting for over an hour.

C   The play lasted for over an hour.

D   It is best as it is.

 The correct answer is <u>C, The play lasted for over an hour</u>. The story is told in the past tense. So the sentence must be in the past tense.

 Put this sentence in the story. Try out the sentence in each place. Pick the place where it makes the most sense.

Sample B

It was the best performance we had ever put on.

F   after sentence 1

G   after sentence 2

H   after sentence 3

J   after sentence 4

 The correct answer is <u>J, after sentence 4</u>. This sentence sums up the story. It goes best at the end.

Answers

SA   Ⓐ Ⓑ Ⓒ Ⓓ

24   SB   Ⓕ Ⓖ Ⓗ Ⓙ

Directions: Here is a story a student wrote about her vacation. She made some mistakes. Read the story carefully. Then read each question. Darken the circle for the correct answer.

1. My parents told me that we were going on a trip for spring vacation. 2. We were going to Disney World. 3. It was going to be a long car ride. 4. I couldn't believe it! 5. I know we were going to have a wonderful time. 6. I couldn't wait to go on Space Mountain. 7. It is supposed to be the scariest roller coaster ride. 8. This was going to be the most exciting vacation of my life.

1 Which best combines sentences 1 and 2 into one sentence?

A My parents told me Disney World was our spring vacation trip.

B For spring vacation, my parents are going to Disney World.

C Going on a trip for spring vacation, my parents told me it was to Disney World.

D My parents told me that we were going on a trip to Disney World for spring vacation.

2 Which is the best way to write sentence 5?

F I could know we were going to have a wonderful time.

G I have known we were going to have a wonderful time.

H I knew we were going to have a wonderful time.

J It is best as it is.

3 Which sentence does <u>not</u> belong in the paragraph?

A sentence 3

B sentence 4

C sentence 5

D sentence 6

Answers

1 Ⓐ Ⓑ Ⓒ Ⓓ   3 Ⓐ Ⓑ Ⓒ Ⓓ

2 Ⓕ Ⓖ Ⓗ Ⓙ

Directions: Choose the word that belongs in the blank. Darken the circle for the correct answer.

Sample

After Natasha sang the song, everyone _____.

A clap

B claps

C clapped

D clapping

Directions: Here is a report about Joe Montana. He was a professional football quarterback for many years. There are some mistakes in the report. Read it carefully, then read each question. Darken the circle for the correct answer.

JOE MONTANA

¹· When Joe Montana was in junior high school, he plays football and basketball and ran track. ²· After basketball practice, he took the school bus home. ³· The bus dropped him off at 5:30. ⁴· One day after practice, some of his teammates wanted to get some food before catching the bus. ⁵· So missed the bus and had to find another way home. ⁶· That meant he didn't arrive on time.

Answers
S Ⓐ Ⓑ Ⓒ Ⓓ

1 **Choose the best way to write sentence 1.**

  A In junior high school, Joe Montana plays football, and basketball and ran track.

  B When Joe Montana was in junior high school, he played football and basketball and ran track.

  C When Joe Montana be in junior high school, he plays football, and basketball and ran track.

  D It is best as it is.

2 **Choose the best way to combine sentences 2 and 3.**

  F After basketball practice, he always took the school bus home at 5:30.

  G The bus dropped him off at basketball practice at 5:30.

  H After basketball practice at 5:30, he took the school bus home.

  J After basketball practice, the school bus dropped him home at 5:30.

3 **Choose the best way to write sentence 5.**

  A So he missed the bus and had to find another way home.

  B Missed the bus and having to find another way home.

  C So we missed the bus and had to find another way home.

  D It is best as it is.

4 **Choose the best way to write sentence 6.**

  F He didn't arrive on time that meant.

  G That meant him didn't arriving on time.

  H That meant him didn't arrive on time.

  J It is best as it is.

Answers

1	Ⓐ Ⓑ Ⓒ Ⓓ	3	Ⓐ Ⓑ Ⓒ Ⓓ
2	Ⓕ Ⓖ Ⓗ Ⓙ	4	Ⓕ Ⓖ Ⓗ Ⓙ

Directions: Here is the second paragraph of the report.

¹· It never occurred to Joe that his parents would be worried. ²· His father called the school. ³· When they told him no one was there, he got worried. ⁴· He come looking for Joe and, not finding him, called home. ⁵· Joe still wasn't there. ⁶· When his dad came back to the house, Joe was already home.

5 Choose the best way to combine sentences 2 and 3.

A When they told him no one was there, his father called the school and got worried.

B His father called the school, telling them that no one was there and getting them worried.

C His father called the school, and when they told him no one was there, he got worried.

D No one was there, so his father called the school and got worried.

6 Choose the best way to write sentence 4.

F He comes looking for Joe and, not finding him, called home.

G He came looking for Joe and, not finding him, called home.

H He come look for Joe and, not finding him, called home.

J He come looked for Joe and, not finding him, called home.

Answers
5 Ⓐ Ⓑ Ⓒ Ⓓ
28 **6** Ⓕ Ⓖ Ⓗ Ⓙ

Directions: Here is the third paragraph of the report.

1. Parents wanted to know why Joe did not call them. 2. They were home all afternoon. 3. Joe told them he had no money. 4. They gave him some change to carry in his shoe. 5. Then he always have money to call them. 6. Joe never forgot what his parents taught him. 7. He knew they loved him and cared about him.

7 Choose the best way to write sentence 1.

  A His parents want to know why Joe did not call them.

  B Parents want to know why Joe did not call them.

  C His parents wanted to know why Joe did not call them.

  D It is best as it is.

8 Choose the best way to write sentence 5.

  F Then he always had money to call them.

  G To call them, he always have money.

  H Then he always has money to call them.

  J It is best as it is.

9 Which sentence does not belong in the paragraph?

  A sentence 1

  B sentence 2

  C sentence 6

  D sentence 7

Answers
7 Ⓐ Ⓑ Ⓒ Ⓓ   9 Ⓐ Ⓑ Ⓒ Ⓓ
8 Ⓕ Ⓖ Ⓗ Ⓙ

Directions: Here is a passage about kangaroos. Read this passage. Then read each question. Darken the circle for the correct answer.

Kangaroos

Have you ever heard of "roos"? If you lived in Australia, you would know that this word refers to kangaroos. The kangaroo is the national animal of Australia. Its likeness is found on the money, stamps, and national seal of Australia.

The kangaroo belongs to a family known as marsupials. Most female marsupials have pouches in which their young grow and develop. Kangaroos are the largest marsupials.

In some parts of Australia there are kangaroo crossing signs. Kangaroos are not careful when they cross roads, and every year thousands are killed by cars. The Australian government protects kangaroos by passing laws against killing these native animals.

10 Choose the sentence that is written correctly.

   F   Kangaroos living in Australia.

   G   There is some kangaroos in the United States.

   H   Most of them lives in zoos.

   J   That is the best place to go see one.

Choose the words that belong in the blanks.

> Once a year we take my pet kangaroo to the __(11)__. We want to make sure that he stays __(12)__.

11 **A**   veterinarian

     B   hospital

     C   scientist

     D   school

12 **F**   large

     G   quick

     H   young

     J   healthy

Answers
10 Ⓕ Ⓖ Ⓗ Ⓙ   **12** Ⓕ Ⓖ Ⓗ Ⓙ
30 **11** Ⓐ Ⓑ Ⓒ Ⓓ

Reading and Language Arts

Directions: Read each sample. Darken the circle for the correct answer. Remember to use the answer sheet on page 109 to fill in your answers.

Sample A

Katrina is very excited about going camping with her cousins, Gary and Linda. The cousins are good friends. The campers plan to travel to the Grand Canyon where they will stay for two weeks.

On their trip the three cousins most likely will

A   be very bored

B   fight and argue

C   have an enjoyable time

D   not talk to one another

Sample B

Directions: Here is a report about elephants. There are some mistakes in the report. Read it carefully, then read the question. Darken the circle for the correct answer.

> 1. I find elephants very interesting. 2. Their trunk is so long that it weighs about 300 pounds. 3. Elephants use their trunk to smell. 4. They also use their trunk to hold things. 5. The trunk working almost like a hand.

Choose the best way to write sentence 5.

F   The trunk works almost like a hand.

G   The trunk work almost like a hand.

H   The trunk worked almost like a hand.

J   It is best as it is.

NATURE'S WAY

Often we do not stop and notice the wonderful things the world around us has to offer.

In this part you will read about something that takes place every day: how plants grow. You will also read about an unusual animal, the flying squirrel.

Directions: Here are some directions on how to grow potatoes. Read these directions carefully. Then read each question. Darken the circle for the correct answer.

Pot of Potatoes

Potatoes are grown in fields, because each seed potato needs a lot of space to develop into a new potato plant. But if you don't have a field, you can grow potatoes in a pot! Plant them in the spring.

You will need: 10-inch (25-cm) flowerpot
                       stones
                       potting soil
                       newspaper
                       water
                       potato

1. Leave a potato to sprout — this will take a couple of weeks. Then put the sprouting potato in a warm, light place. When the shoots are about $\frac{3}{4}$ inch (2 cm) long, the potato is ready to plant. Leave two shoots on one side of the potato, and rub off all the others.

2. Put a few stones in the bottom of the flowerpot, and half-fill it with potting soil. Make a hole for the potato to fit in. Plant it with the shoots pointing up. Cover the rest of the potato with soil and water it. Make sure the soil stays damp while the shoots are growing.

3. After about four weeks, green shoots will poke through the soil. Add more soil and don't forget to water. Keep adding soil as the green shoots appear, until the pot is full.

4. Keep watering the potato plant as it grows leaves and then flowers. When the plant has finished flowering, you must stop watering it. Otherwise the new potatoes in the soil will rot. As the soil dries out, the plant will die. Now is the time to harvest your crop.

5. Put some newspaper on the floor and tip the pot out. Have you grown enough potatoes for supper?

1 Step 1 says the potato is ready to plant when the <u>shoots</u> are $\frac{3}{4}$ inch long. <u>Shoots</u> are

   A   stones

   B   baby potatoes

   C   small plant stems

   D   green flowers

2 Step 4 says that you should keep watering the potato plant until

   F   the soil dries out

   G   the plant grows leaves

   H   the last flower has grown

   J   the first flower appears

3 **This picture shows**

   A   when it's time to add more soil

   B   when it's time to stop watering the plant

   C   when it's time to harvest the potatoes

   D   when it's time to start watering the plant

4 **This passage is mostly about**

   F   how to plant in the spring

   G   how to grow potatoes in a pot

   H   how to grow flowers

   J   how to take care of plants

5 **Step 5 is mostly about**

   A being neat

   B putting newspaper on the floor

   C harvesting your crop

   D tipping the pot

6 **Soil is important because it**

   F waters the plant

   G helps the plant grow

   H dries out the plant

   J fills up the pot

7 **Choose the sentence that is written correctly.**

   A Potatoes in a pot.

   B The shoots grow through the soil.

   C While the shoots are growing.

   D When the plant has finished flowering.

8 **Choose the word that belongs in the blank for <u>both</u> sentences.**

What _____ of potatoes do you like best?

He is very _____ to me.

   F interesting

   G helpful

   H sort

   J kind

9 **Find the sentence that best completes the story.**

> It was the tastiest meal we ever had. _____. Every time Dad walked out of the kitchen, he was carrying something good.

   A We had turkey with stuffing and mashed potatoes.

   B It took me all day to cook it.

   C The next day we ate the leftovers.

   D Cooking is my favorite hobby.

10 **Choose the sentence that has the correct capitalization and punctuation.**

F don't forget to keep the plant warm?

G Be careful not to break the stems!

H Why did you water the plant so much.

J leave two shoots on one side of the potato.

11 **Choose the sentence that best combines both sentences into one.**

The fence keeps animals out of the yard.

It is a small yard.

A The fence keeps animals out of the yard, and the yard is small, too.

B The fence keeps animals out of the small yard.

C The fence keeps small animals out the of yard.

D The fence keeps animals out of the yard, the yard is small.

12 **Which sentences best support this topic sentence?**

I always enjoy working in my garden.

F Seeds cost a lot of money. And birds often fly in and dig them up.

G Most of the things I grow take too much work. Sometimes, I just don't want to be bothered.

H I love vegetables. They taste better when you grow them yourself.

J The fresh air makes me feel good. I love to watch my plants grow.

Directions: Here is a story about an amazing animal. Read this story carefully. Then read each question. Darken the circle for the correct answer.

Flying Squirrels

Can squirrels fly? Of course not! The only mammal that can fly is the bat. But there are animals called flying squirrels. These squirrels do not have wings; however, they glide through the air so well, it looks like they are flying.

The North American flying squirrels are cute and furry. Their eyes are large and dark. This helps them to see at night, which is when they look for food. Nuts and seeds are what they like best. Flying squirrels live in groups in empty trees and birdhouses. They almost never descend to the ground.

How do these animals fly? Thin flaps of skin are stretched between the squirrel's front and hind legs. As the squirrel pushes off from a branch, it spreads its flaps wide. This lets it glide on the air like a parachute. The squirrel can coast gracefully on air currents from tree to tree. Its long, flat tail helps it steer. Flying squirrels can "fly" long distances. They have been known to soar more than one hundred feet between the branches of trees.

Believe it or not, it's all true!

13 **Where do flying squirrels live?**

    A in hollow trees

    B on the ground

    C in holes in the ground

    D on parachutes

14 **What allows the squirrels to fly?**

    F large, dark eyes

    G thin flaps of skin

    H tree branches

    J long, flat tails

15 **Flying squirrels almost never <u>descend</u> to the ground.**

    A word that means the boxed(opposite) of <u>descend</u> is

    A climb

    B drop

    C swoop

    D go down

16 **This story is mostly about**

    F how squirrels can fly

    G gliding like a parachute

    H how to fly without wings

    J a different kind of squirrel

17 These squirrels fly long distances because they know how to use

   A tree branches

   B air currents

   C their wings

   D their front legs

18 Which one of the following "flies" most like a flying squirrel?

   F an airplane

   G a bat

   H a paper airplane

   J a bird

19 Choose the word that is the simple predicate of the sentence.

<u>Squirrels</u> <u>glide</u> fast between the <u>tall</u> <u>trees</u>.

     A   **B**   **C** **D**

20 Choose the word that belongs in the blank.

The parachute lifted and _____ through the air.

   F swoop

   G swoops

   H swooped

   J swooping

21 Choose the word or words that belong in the blank.

Flying squirrels see _____ at night than people.

   A good

   B more good

   C better

   D best

Directions: Choose the words that belong in the blanks.

I was so __(22)__ on my first day of school. I __(23)__ home to tell my father all about the fun I had.

22 **F** true

    G excited

    H sad

    J lonely

23 **A** smiled

    B sang

    C crawled

    D rushed

Part 2

Children's Stories

Every child has a story to tell. This part includes
a lot of stories. Some are about fictional children
and some are about real children.

Directions: Here is a story about a small boy who helps save a whale. Read this story. Then read each question. Darken the circle for the correct answer.

A Thousand Pails of Water

by Ronald Roy

Yukio lived in a fishing village where people fished to make their living. One day he saw a whale that had become lodged between some rocks and was left behind when the tide went out.

The large tail beat the sand, helplessly. The eye, as big as Yukio's hand, rolled in fright. Yukio knew that the whale would not live long out of the sea.

"I will help you, sir," he said. But how? The whale was huge, like a temple. Yukio raced to the water's edge. Was the tide coming in or going out? In, he decided.

The sun was hot on Yukio's back as he stood looking at the whale. Yukio filled his pail with water and threw it over the great head.

"You are so big and my pail is so small!" he cried. "But I will throw a thousand pails of water over you before I stop."

The second pail went on the head as well, and the third and fourth. But Yukio knew he must wet every part of the whale or it would die in the sun.

Yukio made many trips to the sea for water, counting as he went. He threw four pails on the body, then four on the tail, and then three on the head.

There was a little shade on one side of the big gray prisoner. Yukio sat there, out of breath, his heart pounding. Then he looked in the whale's eye and remembered his promise.

Yukio went back to the sea and stopped to fill his pail. How many had he filled so far? He had lost count. But he knew he must not stop.

tide = the rise and fall of the level of the water in the ocean

Yukio fell, the precious water spilling from his pail. He cried, and his tears disappeared into the sand. A wave touched his foot, as if to say, "Get up and carry more water. I am coming, but I am very slow."

Yukio filled his pail over and over. His back hurt, and his arms—but he threw and threw. He fell again, but this time he did not get up.

Yukio felt himself being lifted.

"You have worked hard, little one. Now let us help."

Yukio's grandfather laid him in the shade of one of the rocks. Yukio watched his grandfather throw his first pail of water and go for another.

"Hurry!" Yukio wanted to scream, for his grandfather was old and walked slowly. Then Yukio heard the voices. His father and the village people were running toward the sea. They carried pails and buckets and anything that would hold water.

Some of the villagers removed their jackets and soaked them in the sea. These they placed on the whale's burning skin. Soon the whale was wet all over.

Slowly the sea came closer and closer. At last it covered the huge tail. The village people ran back and forth carrying water, shouting to each other. Yukio knew the whale would be saved.

Yukio's father came and stood by him. "Thank you, Father," Yukio said, "for bringing the village people to help."

"You are strong and good," his father said. "But to save a whale many hands must carry the water."

Now the whale was moving with each new wave. Suddenly a great one lifted him free of the rocks. He was still for a moment, then, with a flip of his tail, he swam out to sea.

24 This passage is mostly about

    F   a fishing village

    G   saving a whale

    H   a day at the shore

    J   a boy and his father

25 Why was the whale frightened?

    A   He knew he could die.

    B   He was afraid of Yukio.

    C   He was scared of the water being thrown at him.

    D   He thought he might drown.

26 Which picture shows that Yukio needed help?

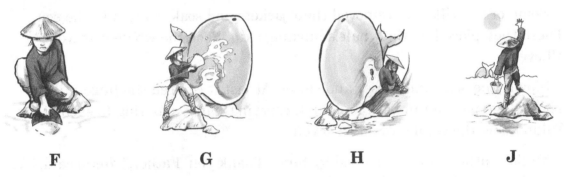

    F   **G**   **H**   **J**

27 What did Yukio mean when he said, "I will throw a thousand pails of water over you before I stop"?

    A   He will not throw any more than a thousand pails of water.

    B   He will throw water on the whale's body.

    C   He will not stop throwing water on the whale until it is saved.

    D   He will soon stop throwing water on the whale.

28 Yukio wanted to scream at his grandfather because

    F   his grandfather was old

    G   Yukio was angry

    H   Yukio wanted to be left alone

    J   his grandfather was too slow

29 Why did the villagers cover the whale with their jackets?

    A   so he would not get cold

    B   so he would not get wet

    C   to keep him wet

    D   to keep him hot

30 How did the whale finally get free?

    F   The tide came in and swept the whale free.

    G   The villagers pushed the whale out.

    H   Yukio set him free.

    J   The whale freed himself with his tail.

31 Yukio lived in Japan. He thought the whale was huge, like a temple. If you were explaining the size of the whale, what might you say?

    A   huge, like a horse

    B   huge, like a house

    C   huge, like a bicycle

    D   huge, like a table

32 **Choose the sentence that is written correctly.**

   F   He walk along the shore.

   G   Yukio seen his grandfather.

   H   He really cared about the whale.

   J   Yukio know that the whale would be saved.

33 **Choose the sentence that best combines both sentences into one.**

Yukio saw the whale stuck in the rocks.

He threw a pail of water on the whale.

   A   Seeing the whale stuck in the rocks, he threw a pail of water on Yukio.

   B   Throwing a pail of water on the whale, Yukio saw that it was stuck in the rocks.

   C   Yukio saw the whale stuck in the rocks, threw a pail of water on the whale.

   D   Yukio threw a pail of water on the whale stuck in the rocks.

34 **Choose the sentence that best completes the story.**

> I like to go fishing. Sometimes my mother and I go out in a boat. _____.

   F   But usually we just fish off the dock.

   G   I like to go boating.

   H   My mother makes the best fried catfish.

   J   I wish we had our own boat.

Directions: Choose the words that belong in the blanks. Darken the circle for the correct answer.

35 The pail of water was too heavy for _____.

    A he

    B him

    C they

    D I

Dear Chizuko,
                                                                (36)

    Since we moved to **(37)** , I have made a lot of friends. However, no one is as much fun to be with as you are. I can't wait until you come to visit me.

                                                      Your best friend,

                                                      Sawako

36 **F** December, 19, 2005

    G December, 19 2005

    H December 19, 2005

    J December 19 2005

37 **A** Portland, oregon

    B Portland, Oregon

    C Portland Oregon

    D portland, Oregon

38 **Choose the sentence that is written correctly.**

    F Far larger than any land animal.

    G Living in cold water.

    H The whale breathes through its blowhole.

    J Swims in the cold ocean waters.

Directions: Here is a story about two sisters. Read this story. Then read each question. Darken the circle for the correct answer.

I Have a Sister; My Sister Is Deaf

adapted from a story by Jeanne Whitehouse Peterson

I have a younger sister. My sister is deaf. She is special. There are not many sisters like mine.

My sister can play the piano, and as she plays, she likes to feel the deep rumbling music. But she will never be able to sing with the piano because she cannot hear the tune.

My sister can dance with another person or march in a line. She likes to leap, to skip, to roll, and to climb to the top of the monkey bars. She watches me as we climb, and I watch her, too. Although she cannot hear me shout, "Look out!" she can see me swinging her way, and then she laughs and swings backward, trying to catch my legs.

I have a sister who likes to go with me out to the grassy lot behind our house. Today we are stalking deer, and when I turn to say something to her, I use no voice, just my fingers and my lips.

My sister understands what I say and walks behind me, stepping where I step. I listen for small sounds, and she watches for quick movements in the grass. My sister is smart.

39 Which word best describes the younger sister?

A boring

B quiet

C musical

D active

40 As the younger sister plays the piano, she

F hears the tune

G feels the music

H sings along

J likes to dance

41 Use this web to answer the question.

1
dance with someone

2
march in line

My Sister Can

3
climb the monkey bars

4
hear someone shout

Which box does <u>not</u> belong?

A   Box 1

B   Box 2

C   Box 3

D   Box 4

42 When the older sister wants to go bike riding, the younger sister most likely

F   goes with her

G   is afraid to go

H   shakes her head "No"

J   watches her older sister

43 One day the two sisters were <u>stalking</u> deer.

What does the word <u>stalking</u> mean?

A   following quietly

B   running after

C   listening for

D   watching

Choose the words that belong in the blanks.

My sister can play soccer better than anyone else on her __(44)__.
When I watch her __(45)__, I am so proud that she is my sister.

44 F   school

G   team

H   family

J   sport

45 A   games

B   balls

C   sports

D   feet

Directions: Here is a story about a boy who gets a little help with his writing. Read this story. Then read each question. Darken the circle for the correct answer.

A Real Whopper

Cal groaned. Mr. Losetti was passing out paper. They were going to have to write compositions. "Now," said Mr. Losetti. "The subject is, 'What I Did During Spring Break.'" Cal looked around. Margaret had already started writing. She was scribbling away. "Something wrong?" said Mr. Losetti.

Cal looked up. "I don't know what to write," he said and shrugged helplessly.

"Ah!" said Mr. Losetti. "Yes, compositions. They give you trouble. Well, come with me."

Cal followed Mr. Losetti up to his desk. "Here," said Mr. Losetti, handing Cal a really fancy pen. "This will help. It's a magic pen. Go ahead. Give it a try."

Cal went back to his seat and studied the pen. "Oh, please!" whispered Angela who sat behind him. "Not that stupid magic pen scam again!" She snorted.

Cal turned around. "What do you mean?"

"It's phony. That pen's not magic. Losetti only wants you to think it is. It's his way of getting you to believe you can write."

"You mean the pen can't do anything?" said Cal.

"Nope. But this," said Angela, withdrawing a chewed up pencil from her knapsack, "is the real thing."

"What does it do?"

"It tells lies."

"Lies?" said Cal.

"Yup. Real whoppers. What did you do on spring break?"

"Not much," said Cal.

"Well, this is just what you need, then," said Angela, and she handed Cal the pencil. "Go on. Give it a shot."

A few days later . . .

"Wow!" said Mr. Losetti when Cal handed back the composition. "What a composition! You were captured by aliens, huh? That must have been quite an adventure. I doubt anybody can top that."

"Oh yeah?" said Angela. "I bet I can."

"Really?" said Mr. Losetti.

"Yup." She winked at Cal. "Just give me a minute to find a pencil."

46 **Why did Cal groan when he realized he had to write a composition?**

   F   He had left his lucky pen home.

   G   He had trouble writing.

   H   He felt too sick to write.

   J   Everyone made fun of his writing.

47 **What was really special about Mr. Losetti's pen?**

   A   It was very expensive.

   B   It was magic.

   C   Very few students were allowed to use it.

   D   Nothing.

48 **What did Mr. Losetti hope would happen when he gave Cal the pen?**

   F   He hoped Cal would do magic tricks with it.

   G   He hoped it would improve Cal's penmanship.

   H   He hoped Cal would find it easier to write his composition.

   J   He hoped Cal would trade it for Angela's pencil.

49 **In what way was Angela's pencil similar to Mr. Losetti's pen?**

   A   They were both very old.

   B   They both had magical powers.

   C   Neither one was magic.

   D   Neither one had ever been used before.

50 **What did using Angela's pencil help Cal to do?**

   F   get rid of Mr. Losetti's pen

   G   come up with an idea for his composition

   H   get out of writing a composition

   J   remember that he got captured by aliens

51 **From where did Cal get the idea to write about aliens?**

    A   his own experience

    B   the pencil

    C   Angela

    D   his own imagination

52 **Which best describes the theme of this story?**

    F   Believe in yourself and you can do it.

    G   All writers are liars.

    H   You never know who has a secret.

    J   Don't do something you don't want to do.

53 **Choose the sentence that is written correctly.**

    A   Cal did not wanted to write a composition.

    B   Cal did not use the pen Mr. Losetti gives him.

    C   The pencil from Angela worked better.

    D   Writing is not hard work when you has a story to tell.

Directions: Hakim's teacher has asked the class to write about a trip they have taken. To help the students write their stories, the teacher designed a checklist. Read the checklist. Then read each question. Darken the circle for the correct answer.

A Trip I Took

1. Name _____

2. Where I went _____

3. When I went _____

4. Who went with me _____

5. What are some things that happened on the trip?
   The things can be funny, strange, or just interesting.

   _____

   _____

   _____

6. How did you feel about the trip?
   Come up with at least three words you could use to describe the trip.

   _____

   _____

   _____

54 Hakim decided to write about his trip to Washington, D.C. He chose that trip because he loved visiting the White House. Where should he write about what happened on his visit to the White House?

F in Part 2

G in Part 3

H in Part 4

J in Part 5

55 Which word or words would Hakim most likely write in Part 6?

A amazed

B Mom

C in the summer

D Washington, D.C.

56 How will the checklist help Hakim?

F It will help him come up with a title.

G It will help him write about himself.

H It will help him arrange his thoughts.

J It will help him with his spelling.

Directions: Here is the first paragraph of Hakim's story. He made some mistakes. Read it carefully, then read each question. Darken the circle for the correct answer.

Hakim's Story

1. I could not sleep. 2. It was the night before my trip. 3. I was going to Washington, D.C. 4. I had always dreamed of going to our nation's capital. 5. That are where the President lives.

57 **Choose the best way to combine sentences 1 and 2.**

A Before my trip I could not sleep because it was the night.

B Before my trip was the night I could not sleep.

C I could not sleep because it was the night before my trip.

D I could not sleep, it was the night before my trip.

58 **Choose the best way to write sentence 5.**

F That is where the President lives.

G That was where the President lives.

H That are where the President living.

J It is best as it is.

Directions: Here is the second paragraph of Hakim's story.

1. I arrived in Washington, D.C., on a beautiful day. 2. The sun shining brightly. 3. My first stop was at the White House. 4. The President was not in, but I got to see where he lives. 5. After that, I went to the United States Mint, where they print paper money.

59 **Choose the best way to write sentence 2.**

A The sun shone brightly.

B The sun shines brightly.

C The sun shine brightly.

D It is best as it is.

60 **Choose the best way to write sentence 4.**

F The President is not in, but I got to see where he lives.

G The President are not in, but I got to see where he lives.

H The President be not in, but I got to see where he lives.

J It is best as it is.

Directions: Here is the third paragraph of Hakim's story.

1. The next day I visited other important places. 2. First stop was the Capitol Building. 3. I heard senators talking about a new law. 4. I was so hungry that I ate my lunch in the park.

61 **Which sentence does not belong in the paragraph?**

A sentence 1

B sentence 2

C sentence 3

D sentence 4

62 **Choose the best way to write sentence 2.**

F His first stop was the Capitol Building.

G Stopping first was the Capitol Building.

H My first stop was the Capitol Building.

J It is best as it is.

63 **Which sentence is the best ending to Hakim's story?**

A I had a hot dog and a coke.

B I was having so much fun, I did not want to go home.

C The next day I was going to the Vietnam Memorial.

D It was going to be a long ride home.

Directions: Here is a story about George Lucas. He has made such popular films as *Star Wars* and *Raiders of the Lost Ark*. George was as clever as a child as he is now as an adult. Read about some of the things he did when he was young. Then read each question. Darken the circle for the correct answer.

A Talented Young Man

What do you think the creator of *Star Wars* did for fun when he was growing up? Would you expect that he built a fantasy world to play in? Well, George Lucas was an imaginative child. He did not just sit around doing nothing all day. Even as a young boy he liked to create things that entertained people. George's childhood friend Mel remembers one of the fun projects he helped George with. "One summer we made a haunted house in my parents' garage." Of course, the house had all kinds of special scary effects rigged up by George. The house was so spooky that even though they charged admission to go in, neighborhood kids stood in line to see it!

George created another kind of make-believe world for his friend Janet. This one was a dollhouse designed to fit her Madame Alexander doll. Out of a cardboard box, George created a house with wallpaper on the walls and furniture in every room. Janet's doll could sit on a sofa made from a milk carton and read by the light of a lipstick-tube lamp.

Like the characters of his movies, young George loved excitement. One place where he could find the thrills he adored was in Disneyland. One summer he and Mel "published" a newspaper called *The Weekly Bugle*. In each edition was a story by George about one of the rides at Disneyland.

George was entranced by the adventure shows found on Saturday afternoon television. These shows inspired him to make one of his first movies, which was done in Mel's backyard. With an eight-millimeter movie camera, the two boys filmed a war movie complete with special effects. Those adventure shows were also the idea behind George's *Indiana Jones* movies created years later.

As he got older, George's imagination and talent continued to grow. He took art in high school; however, his teachers were not always thrilled by his work. One classmate remembers a drawing of armored space soldiers with weapons. When George's art teacher saw it, she said, "Oh George, get serious!" Luckily for us, George didn't take her seriously and went on to make one of the most loved science fiction movies of all time.

64 This story is mostly about

F George Lucas's friendship with Mel

G when George Lucas was a child

H how *Star Wars* was developed

J the first special effects

65 How did George make money when he was a child?

A by selling newspapers

B by making toys

C by entertaining other children

D by making movies

66 Which word best describes George Lucas as a child?

F dull

G gloomy

H inventive

J moody

67 Which sentence from the story supports your answer to question 66?

A He did not just sit around doing nothing all day.

B Out of a cardboard box, George created a house with wallpaper on the walls and furniture in every room.

C Like the characters in his movies, George loved excitement.

D Those adventure shows were also the idea behind George's *Indiana Jones* movies created years later.

68 According to the story, what did George write about in *The Weekly Bugle*?

F the rides at an amusement park

G his haunted house

H the story for *Indiana Jones*

J the adventures that he and Mel had

69 George was <u>entranced</u> by the adventure shows found on Saturday afternoon television.

A word that means the opposite of <u>entranced</u> is

A delighted

B bored

C excited

D saddened

70 What is something you can learn from this biography?

F If at first you don't succeed, try, try again.

G Practice makes perfect.

H Be all that you can be.

J Follow your heart and you will succeed.

Directions: This story is about a real family of black pioneers. They left their home in Kentucky for some free land in Kansas. Read this story. Then read each question. Darken the circle for the correct answer.

Wagon Wheels

by Barbara Brenner

"There it is, boys," Daddy said. "Across this river is Nicodemus, Kansas. That is where we are going to build our house. There is free land for everyone here in the West. All we have to do is go and get it."

We had come a long way to get to Kansas. All the way from Kentucky. It had been a hard trip, and a sad one. Mama died on the way. Now there were just the four of us — Daddy, Willie, Little Brother, and me.

We crossed the river, wagon and all. A man was waiting for us on the other side. "I am Sam Hickman," he said. "Welcome to the town of Nicodemus."

"Why, thank you, Brother," Daddy said. "But where is your town?"

"Right here," Mr. Hickman said.

We did not see any houses. But we saw smoke coming out of holes in the prairie. "Shucks!" Daddy said. "Holes in the ground are for rabbits and snakes, not for free black people. I am a carpenter. I can build fine wood houses for this town."

"No time to build wood houses now," Mr. Hickman told Daddy. "Winter is coming. And winter in Kansas is mean. Better get yourself a dugout before the ground freezes."

Daddy knew Mr. Hickman was right. We got our shovels, and we dug us a dugout. It wasn't much of a place — dirt floor, dirt walls, no windows. And the roof was just grass and branches. But we were glad to have that dugout when the wind began to whistle across the prairie.

Winter came. And that Kansas winter was mean. It snowed day after day. We couldn't hunt or fish. We had no more rabbit stew, and no more fish fresh from the river. All we had to eat was cornmeal mush.

Then one day there was no more cornmeal. There was not a lick of food in the whole town of Nicodemus. There was nothing left to burn for firewood. Little Brother cried all the time — he was cold and hungry. Daddy wrapped blankets around him. "Hush, baby son," he said. "Try to sleep. The supply train will be coming soon." But the supply train did not come — not that day or the next.

On the third day we heard the sound of horses. Daddy looked out to see who it was. "Oh, Lord!" he said. "Indians!" We were so scared. We had all heard stories about Indians. I tried to be brave.

"I will get my gun, Daddy," I said. But Daddy said, "Hold on, Johnny. Wait and see what they do." We watched from the dugout.

Everyone in Nicodemus was watching the Indians. First they made a circle. Then each Indian took something from his saddlebag and dropped it on the ground. The Indians turned and rode straight toward the dugouts. "Now they are coming for us!" Willie cried. We raised our guns. But the Indians rode right past us and kept on going.

We waited a long time to be sure they were gone. Then everyone ran out into the snow to see what the Indians had left. It was FOOD!

There was a feast in Nicodemus that night. But before we ate, Daddy said to us, "Johnny, Willie, Little Brother, I want you to remember this day. When someone says bad things about Indians, tell them the Osage Indians saved our lives in Nicodemus."

71 This story mostly tells about

   A winter in Kansas

   B living in a dugout

   C an American Indian attack

   D a pioneer family

72 Which event happened in the story?

   F The family made a house out of dirt.

   G The father built a fine wood house for his family.

   H The Osage Indians warned the townspeople to leave them alone.

   J The supply train showed up with food and firewood.

73 Which word best describes Johnny's feelings when he saw the Osage Indians?

   A happy

   B frightened

   C brave

   D uninterested

74 Everyone treated the Osage as if they were

   F friends

   G strangers

   H beggars

   J enemies

75 The wind began to whistle across the prairie.

What does <u>the wind began to whistle</u> mean?

   A the wind stopped blowing

   B the wind called them

   C the wind made noise as it blew

   D someone was whistling

76 Which word best describes the father at the end of the story?

   F fearful

   G grateful

   H disappointed

   J dismayed

Directions: Here is a report about Todd Reid, a youth with a golden future. Read this story. Then read each question. Darken the circle for the correct answer.

A Tennis Whiz

1. Todd Reid is a tennis whiz. 2. He is 13 years old. 3. He came from Australia to America to make his fortune. 4. He has won many tennis championships, so he has a bright future. 5. A company that makes tennis racquets, sneakers, and clothes is paying for Todd's education. 6. This company will also pay he to wear their clothing. 7. Of course, everything Todd wears has the name of the company.

77 Choose the best way to combine sentences 1 and 2.

   A A 13-year-old, Todd Reid is a tennis whiz.

   B Todd Reid is a tennis whiz, he is 13 years old.

   C Todd Reid is a 13-year-old tennis whiz.

   D Todd Reid is a tennis whiz for 13 years.

78 Choose the best way to write sentence 6.

   F This company will also pay to wear their clothing.

   G This company will also pay him to wear their clothing.

   H This company will also pay them to wear their clothing.

   J It is best as it is.

Directions: Here is the second paragraph of the report.

^{1.} Some people think that Todd is moved too fast.
^{2.} They think he is much too young for this pressure.
^{3.} Now he lives in a tennis camp where he practices five to seven hours a day. ^{4.} At night he studies.
^{5.} Maybe it's not such a wonderful life, after all!

79 Choose the best way to write sentence 1.

   A Some people think that Todd is moving too fast.

   B Some people think that Todd moves too fast.

   C Some people think that Todd moving too fast.

   D It is best as it is.

80 Choose the best way to write sentence 3.

   F Now he lives in a tennis camp where he practicing five to seven hours a day.

   G Now he lives in a tennis camp where he practiced five to seven hours a day.

   H Now living in a tennis camp where he practicing five to seven hours a day.

   J It is best as it is.

Section
B

Mathematics

About Section B: Mathematics

This section of the book has been developed to refresh basic skills, familiarize your child with test formats and directions, and teach test-taking strategies. This section of the book is divided into three components: Lessons, Review Tests, and Comprehensive Test.

Note: In order to answer some of the problems in this section, students will need a ruler with measurements marked off in both inches and centimeters. A ruler is provided on page 101.

Lessons

There is one lesson for each of the nine math skills assessed on the CTB-TerraNova Mathematics test. Each lesson contains:

- *Try This:* a skill strategy that enables your child to approach each lesson in a logical manner

- *Sample:* to familiarize your child with test-taking items

- *Think It Through:* the correct answer to the sample item and an explanation that tells why the correct answer is correct and why the incorrect answers are wrong

- two practice questions based on the lesson and modeled on the kinds of items found on the CTB-TerraNova

Review Test

The lessons are followed by a short Review Test that covers all the skills in the lessons. This section is designed to provide your child with independent practice that will familiarize him or her with the testing situation.

Comprehensive Test

The last component in this section is a Comprehensive Test. This test gives your child an opportunity to take a test under conditions that parallel those he or she will face when taking the CTB-TerraNova Mathematics test.

In order to simulate the CTB-TerraNova test as closely as possible, we have suggested time limits for the Comprehensive Test. This will enable your child to experience test taking under the same structured conditions that apply when achievement tests are administered. Furthermore, your child will have a final opportunity to apply the skills he or she has learned in this section prior to taking the CTB-TerraNova.

The recommended time limits are:
Part 1: 15 minutes
Part 2: 45 minutes

Have your child use the Mathematics Test Answer Sheet on page 111 to record the answers for this comprehensive test.

Answer Key

The Answer Key at the back of the book contains the answers for all the problems found in this section.

Mathematics

·········· Lesson 1: Number and Number Relations

Directions: Read each question carefully. Darken the circle for the correct answer.

Try This
When reading whole numbers, work from right to left: ones, tens, hundreds, thousands, and so on.

Sample

Which of these is another way to write the number 5,608?

A   five thousands, six hundreds, eight ones

B   five thousands, six hundreds, eight tens

C   five thousands, six tens, eight ones

D   five hundreds, six tens, eight ones

E   None of these

Think It Through
The correct answer is <u>A, five thousands, six hundreds, eight ones</u>. Since there is a zero in the tens place, the answer does not include tens.

---

1   Aaron, Belinda, Cassie, and Dave sold candy bars to raise money for their school trip. The bars below show how many each student sold.

Which list shows the students in order from most to least candy bars sold?

A   Aaron, Belinda, Cassie, Dave

B   Dave, Belinda, Aaron, Cassie

C   Aaron, Belinda, Dave, Cassie

D   Dave, Belinda, Cassie, Aaron

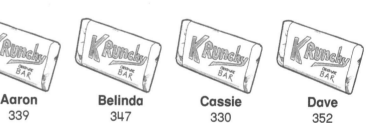

Aaron 339   **Belinda** 347   **Cassie** 330   **Dave** 352

2   An even number of people went to the school concert last night. How many people could have gone?

F   105

G   261

H   376

J   449

Answers
S   Ⓐ Ⓑ Ⓒ Ⓓ Ⓔ   2   Ⓕ Ⓖ Ⓗ Ⓙ
1   Ⓐ Ⓑ Ⓒ Ⓓ

·········· Lesson 2: Computation and Numerical Estimation

Directions: Read each question carefully. Darken the circle for the correct answer.

Read word problems carefully. Look for clue words to help you pick the operations you should use.

Sample

In January Marta earned $47.50 baby-sitting. In February she earned $66.00 baby-sitting. How much did Marta earn baby-sitting during these two months?

A $18.50

B $48.16

C $103.50

D $113.50

E   None of these

The correct answer is <u>D, $113.50</u>. To find the amount earned in all, add the amounts earned in January and February: $47.50 + $66.00 = <u>$113.50</u>.

---

1   Solve.

$$\frac{7}{9}$$
$$-\frac{5}{9}$$

A   2

B $1\frac{1}{3}$

C $\frac{2}{3}$

D $\frac{2}{9}$

2   Robert and his two friends had pizza for lunch. Which is closest to the amount the three boys spent in all?

Robert	$6.25
Paolo	$5.65
Stuart	$4.85

F $15

G $16

H $17

J $18

Answers
S   Ⓐ Ⓑ Ⓒ Ⓓ Ⓔ   2   Ⓕ Ⓖ Ⓗ Ⓙ

1   Ⓐ Ⓑ Ⓒ Ⓓ

Lesson 3: Operation Concepts

Directions: Read each question carefully. Darken the circle for the correct answer.

 Try This Read the directions for the problem carefully. Then try using each of the answer choices in the problem.

Sample

Look at the problem below. Which symbol goes in the box to give the *greatest* answer?

84 ☐ 12

A   +

B   ÷

C   ×

D   −

 **Think It Through**   The correct answer is C, ×. Multiplication leads to an answer of 84 × 12 = 1,008.

---

1   Which number sentence would find the total number of nickels shown?

A   20 − 5 = ☐
B   4 + 5 = ☐
C   4 × 5 = ☐
D   20 ÷ 4 = ☐

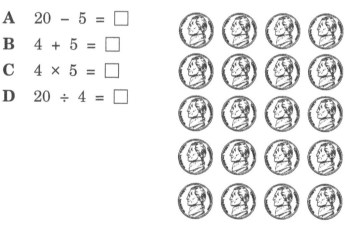

2   Ms. Minson baked a dozen muffins. Her sons ate 4 of them. How many more must they eat so that exactly $\frac{1}{2}$ of the muffins will have been eaten?

F   1

G   2

H   3

J   6

K   None of these

Answers
S   Ⓐ Ⓑ Ⓒ Ⓓ   2   Ⓕ Ⓖ Ⓗ Ⓙ Ⓚ
1   Ⓐ Ⓑ Ⓒ Ⓓ

Lesson 4: Measurement

Directions: Read each question carefully. Darken the circle for the correct answer.

Try This

When counting time on a clock, try to picture the minute hand moving forward. This can help you keep track of minutes and hours.

Sample

The clock shows the time it is now. How many hours and minutes are there until 12 o'clock?

A 4 hours 15 minutes

B 4 hours 45 minutes

C 5 hours 15 minutes

D 5 hours 45 minutes

Think It Through

The correct answer is <u>A, 4 hours 15 minutes</u>. The time on the clock is 7:45. It is 15 minutes until 8 o'clock. It is then 4 hours until 12 o'clock. So, it is 4 hours 15 minutes until 12 o'clock.

---

1 Use the centimeter side of your ruler to solve this problem. What is the length of the shorter side of the rectangle?

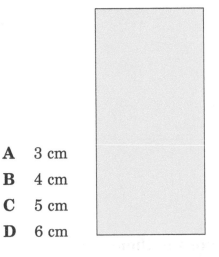

A 3 cm

B 4 cm

C 5 cm

D 6 cm

2 Which weighs the least?

F a 1-ounce weight

G a 1-pound weight

H a 60-pound weight

J a 1-ton weight

Answers

S (A)(B)(C)(D)   2 (F)(G)(H)(J)

70 1 (A)(B)(C)(D)

Directions: Read each question carefully. Darken the circle for the correct answer.

Try This

When you are asked how a figure changes, draw it on paper. Then fold it, turn it, or slide it.

Sample

Tomie flips the letter across the line shown. What figure will result?

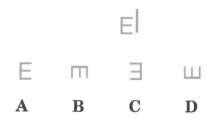

A   **B**   **C**   **D**

Think It Through

The correct answer is C, ∃. When a figure is flipped across a vertical line, left becomes right and right becomes left.

---

1 Which two lines are perpendicular?

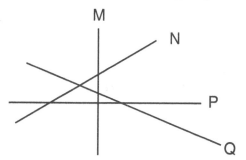

   A M and P

   B M and Q

   C N and P

   D N and Q

2 How many faces does the cube shown have?

   F 3

   G 4

   H 5

   J 6

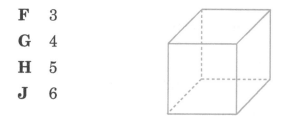

Answers
S   Ⓐ Ⓑ Ⓒ Ⓓ   2   Ⓕ Ⓖ Ⓗ Ⓙ
1   Ⓐ Ⓑ Ⓒ Ⓓ

Directions: Read each question carefully. Darken the circle for the correct answer.

 You can sometimes find out how many ways objects can be combined by making an organized list, step-by-step.

Sample

Eddie's Sweet Shop offers four flavors of ice cream and two sizes of cone. How many different ice cream cones are possible?

A 2
B 6
C 8
D 16

Flavors	Cone Sizes
Vanilla	Small
Chocolate	Large
Strawberry	
Rocky Road	

Think It Through The correct answer is C, 8. You can list all the different cones. Or you can use a tree diagram to find this answer.

Four students ran for school president. The graph below shows the number of votes each student got. Study the graph. Use it to answer problems 1 and 2.

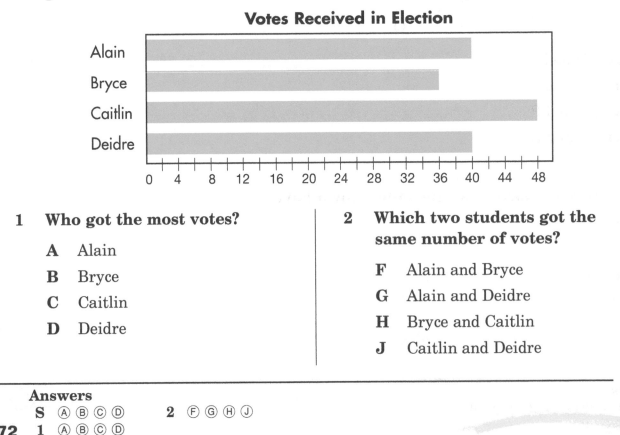

1 Who got the most votes?

  A Alain
  B Bryce
  C Caitlin
  D Deidre

2 Which two students got the same number of votes?

  F Alain and Bryce
  G Alain and Deidre
  H Bryce and Caitlin
  J Caitlin and Deidre

Answers
S Ⓐ Ⓑ Ⓒ Ⓓ   **2** Ⓕ Ⓖ Ⓗ Ⓙ

1 Ⓐ Ⓑ Ⓒ Ⓓ

Lesson 7: Patterns, Functions, and Algebra

Directions: Read each question carefully. Darken the circle for the correct answer.

Try This

This question asks about a pattern. See how you can get from the first number to the next. See if you can use the same rule for the next numbers.

Sample

Look at the pattern below. What number is missing?

20, 28, 36, 44, ____, 60

A 45

B 48

C 50

D 52

Think It Through

The correct answer is <u>D, 52</u>. Each number is gotten by adding 8 to the number before: 44 + 8 = <u>52</u>.

---

1 The number of shaded squares is changing. If the pattern continues, what figure could come next?

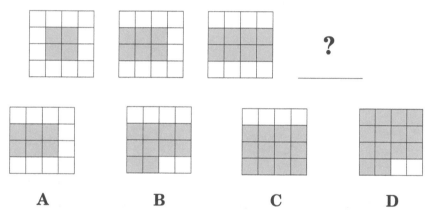

2 The table shows the different prices of a pack of trading cards over the past three summers. If the pattern continues, what will the price be next summer?

F $0.95

G $1.00

H $1.05

J $1.15

Price of Trading Cards	
Two years ago	$0.75
Last year	$0.85
This year	$0.95

Answers

S Ⓐ Ⓑ Ⓒ Ⓓ   2 Ⓕ Ⓖ Ⓗ Ⓙ

1 Ⓐ Ⓑ Ⓒ Ⓓ

Lesson 8: Problem Solving and Reasoning

Directions: Read each question carefully. Darken the circle for the correct answer.

Try This

Test each answer choice given. This will help you get rid of incorrect answers.

Sample

Joseph has an envelope containing dimes, but no other coins. How much could Joseph have in this envelope?

A $0.25

B $1.25

C $2.02

D $4.20

Think It Through

The correct answer is D, $4.20. Since Joseph has only dimes, the total amount must end in a zero.

---

1 In March Bo got a raise of $0.40 more an hour. In April he got a raise of $0.50 more an hour. After that raise, his salary was $9.20 per hour. What was Bo's salary in February?

A $8.30 per hour

B $8.70 per hour

C $9.70 per hour

D $10.10 per hour

2 Since it opened, the Charleston School has sent three students each year to meet the governor. If you wanted to figure out how many students in all the Charleston School has sent to meet the governor, what else must you know?

F how many students go to the Charleston School

G how many students were sent last year

H how many years the Charleston School has been open

J the address of the governor

Answers

S Ⓐ Ⓑ Ⓒ Ⓓ   2 Ⓕ Ⓖ Ⓗ Ⓙ

74 1 Ⓐ Ⓑ Ⓒ Ⓓ

Lesson 9: Communication

Directions: Read each question carefully. Darken the circle for the correct answer.

Try This

Look at the picture carefully. Make sure you understand all the information in it.

Sample

Tasha is 11 years old. How much will it cost for Tasha and her mother to attend a movie?

A $16

B $14

C $8

D $6

Movie Ticket Prices

Children (under age 12) $6

Adults $8

Think It Through

The correct answer is <u>B, $14</u>. Since Tasha is under age 12, she pays $6. Her mother pays $8. In all, they pay $6 + $8 = <u>$14</u>.

---

1   The chart shows the cost of mailing a letter. How much will it cost to mail a letter that weighs 4 ounces?

A $0.32

B $1.01

C $1.24

D $1.28

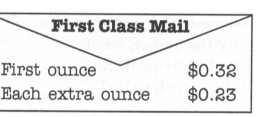

First Class Mail	
First ounce	$0.32
Each extra ounce	$0.23

2   Use the map shown. If Fred starts at the school and walks 3 blocks south, where will he be?

F   at the train station

G   at the playground

H   at home

J   at the deli

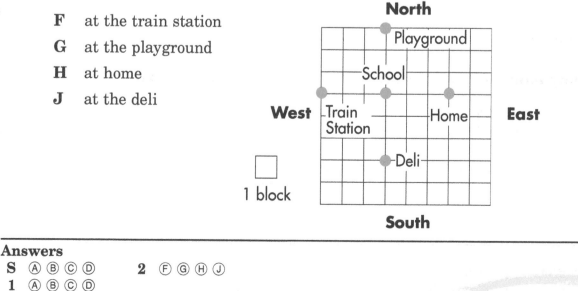

Answers

S Ⓐ Ⓑ Ⓒ Ⓓ   2 Ⓕ Ⓖ Ⓗ Ⓙ

1 Ⓐ Ⓑ Ⓒ Ⓓ

Directions: Read each question. Darken the circle for the correct answer.

Sample

$9 \times 7 =$

A 56

B 72

C 70

D 63

E None of these

---

1 Based on the pattern shown, how many triangles will be shaded in the next picture?

A 7

B 9

C 10

D 12

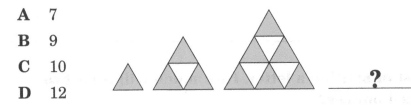

2 At the beginning of the school year, 114 students signed up for a project. By December, 68 of those students had finished their project. How many students still had work to do?

F 46

G 56

H 172

J 182

K None of these

3 How many pairs of congruent figures are there in the picture?

A 1

B 2

C 3

D 4

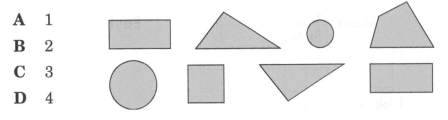

Answers

S Ⓐ Ⓑ Ⓒ Ⓓ Ⓔ   2 Ⓕ Ⓖ Ⓗ Ⓙ Ⓚ

1 Ⓐ Ⓑ Ⓒ Ⓓ   3 Ⓐ Ⓑ Ⓒ Ⓓ

4 Which number sentence could be used to find the total number of cookies?

F   8 + 3 = ___

G 8 − 3 = ___

H 8 × 3 = ___

J   8 ÷ 3 = ___

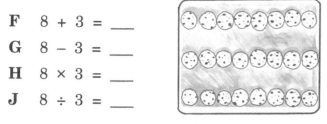

5 Maria bought some food. She got the change shown below from a $10 bill. How much did she spend?

A $9.64

B $9.54

C $8.64

D $8.54

6 Martin remembers watching the Summer Olympics when he was 12 years old, 16 years old, and 20 years old. If this pattern continues, how old will Martin be when he watches the Summer Olympics again?

F 21 years old

G 22 years old

H 24 years old

J 28 years old

7 Which time is the same as the one shown on the first wristwatch?

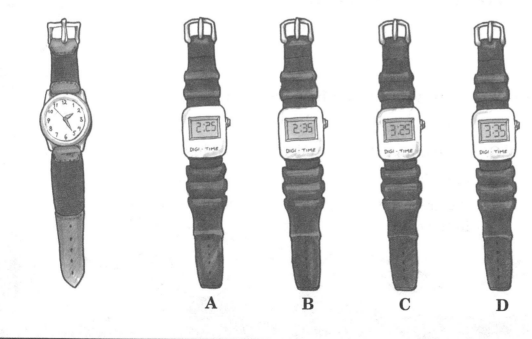

A   B   C   D

Answers

4 Ⓕ Ⓖ Ⓗ Ⓙ   6 Ⓕ Ⓖ Ⓗ Ⓙ

5 Ⓐ Ⓑ Ⓒ Ⓓ   7 Ⓐ Ⓑ Ⓒ Ⓓ

Collection Fun!

Anyone in 3rd grade through 6th grade can join the Berkeley Avenue School Collectors Club. The graph shows how many students are in the club. Study the graph. Then do problems 8 through 10.

Number of Students in Collectors Club

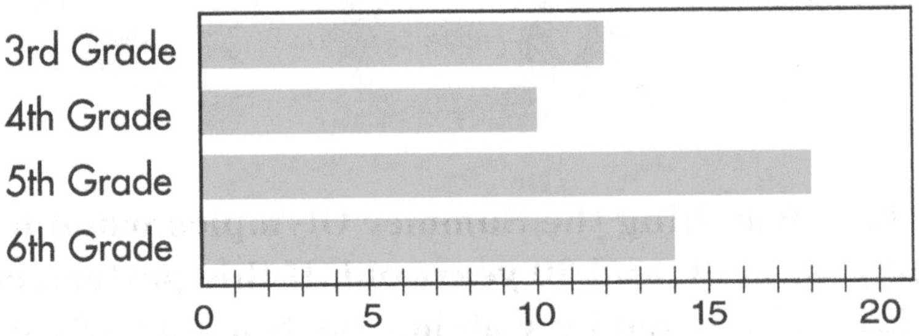

8 **Which grade has the fewest number of students in the Collectors Club?**

F   3rd grade   H   5th grade

G   4th grade   J   6th grade

9 **How many more 5th graders than 6th graders are in the Collectors Club?**

A   1   C   3

B   2   D   4

10 **What can you *not* tell from reading the graph?**

F   the number of 3rd graders in the club

G   the total number of students in the club

H   the total number of 10-year olds in the club

J   the grade with the greatest number of students in the club

Answers

8 (F) (G) (H) (J)   10 (F) (G) (H) (J)

78 9 (A) (B) (C) (D)

11 Santov the Magician told the class, "Think of an even multiple of 3 greater than 20 but less than 30." What number must the class think of?

   A   21

   B   24

   C   27

   D   30

12 What is 3,438 rounded to the nearest hundred?

   F   3,000

   G   3,400

   H   3,440

   J   3,500

   K   None of these

13 Herm has worked for 3 weeks. He wrote down what he earned in a chart.

Week 1	$98
Week 2	$187
Week 3	$312

Which is the best estimate of his total earnings?

   A $500

   B $600

   C $700

   D $800

14 Look at the number sentence below.

12 ___ 4 =

Which operation would lead to the *smallest* result?

   F   ÷

   G   ×

   H   +

   J   −

Answers

11 Ⓐ Ⓑ Ⓒ Ⓓ   13 Ⓐ Ⓑ Ⓒ Ⓓ

12 Ⓕ Ⓖ Ⓗ Ⓙ Ⓚ   14 Ⓕ Ⓖ Ⓗ Ⓙ

15 Dr. Sellers has three workers at her office. Ms. Gillette earns a wage of $20 per hour, Mr. Ruiz earns $16 per hour, and Mr. Scott earns $15 per hour. What is the average wage for the three workers?

   A $18 per hour

   B $17 per hour

   C $16 per hour

   D $15 per hour

Below are four different spinners. Study the spinners. Then use them to answer problems 16 and 17.

Spinner 1   Spinner 2   Spinner 3   Spinner 4

16 On which spinner is the chance of landing on 3 least?

   F   Spinner 1

   G   Spinner 2

   H   Spinner 3

   J   Spinner 4

17 On which spinner is the chance of landing on an even number greatest?

   A   Spinner 1

   B   Spinner 2

   C   Spinner 3

   D   Spinner 4

Answers

15 Ⓐ Ⓑ Ⓒ Ⓓ   **17** Ⓐ Ⓑ Ⓒ Ⓓ

16 Ⓕ Ⓖ Ⓗ Ⓙ

STOP

Directions: Read each question carefully. Darken the circle for the correct answer. Remember to use the answer sheet on page 111 to fill in your answers.

Sample A

$$
\begin{array}{r}
56 \\
+ 34 \\
\hline
\end{array}
$$

A   22

B   32

C   80

D   90

E   None of these

Sample B

Ticket Prices
Adult $8.00
Child $5.50

Mr. Todd bought movie tickets for himself and his three children. How much did he spend in all?

F $22.00

G $24.50

H $29.50

J $32.00

Sample C

Use the inch side of your ruler to solve this problem.

How many inches wide is the photo from edge to edge?

    A   3 inches

    B   4 inches

    C   5 inches

    D   6 inches

1 $7 \times 7 =$

   A 14

   B 42

   C 49

   D 56

   E None of these

2 **109**
  + 686

   F 785

   G 795

   H 885

   J 895

   K None of these

3 $\frac{3}{8} - \frac{1}{8} =$

   A $\frac{1}{8}$

   B $\frac{1}{4}$

   C $\frac{1}{2}$

   D 2

   E None of these

4 $2.34 + 0.6 =$

   F 2.30

   G 2.40

   H 2.94

   J 8.34

   K None of these

5 $200 \times 300 =$

   A 600

   B 6,000

   C 50,000

   D 60,000

   E None of these

6 $683 - 567 =$

   F 126

   G 116

   H 26

   J 16

   K None of these

BATTER'S UP!

A 4th-grade class is doing a social studies project. They are studying their local minor league baseball team, the Boontown Bees. Solve problems 7 through 11.

7   In April 4,512 fans attended Bees games at Faulkner Field. In May 8,839 fans attended games. How many fans attended in both months combined?

   A   12,341

   B   12,351

   C   13,341

   D   13,351

   E   None of these

8   Field-level seats at Faulkner Field are grouped in boxes of four. Twenty-eight students from the school are going to a game next week. If the students want to sit in field-level seats, how many boxes will they buy?

   F   4

   G   6

   H   8

   J   10

   K   None of these

9 The distance from home plate to the left-field wall is 324 feet at Faulkner Field. How far is this distance in yards?

A 27 yards

B 108 yards

C 180 yards

D 972 yards

E None of these

10 Hot dogs cost $2.25 at Faulkner Field. Which number sentence could be used to find the change you would get if you buy a hot dog with a $10 bill?

F $2.25 - 10 = \_\_\_$

G $2.25 + 10 = \_\_\_$

H $10 - 2.25 = \_\_\_$

J $10 \div 2.25 = \_\_\_$

11 The table shows the prices at the gift stand at Faulkner Field. A fan bought two items with a $10 bill and got no change. What did she purchase?

Souvenirs

Yearbook	$6.50
Cap	$7.00
Pennant	$4.00
Photo Set	$3.00
Bat	$10.00
Shirt	$9.00

A a yearbook and a pennant

B a cap and a photo set

C a bat and a shirt

D a pennant and two photo sets

Directions: Use estimation to solve problems 12 through 14.

12 Which of these is the best estimate of 423 × 99 = ___ ?

    F   420,000

    G   42,000

    H   4,200

    J   420

13 The table below shows what Sal made over the past three weekends.

Sal's Earnings

$130.45

$124.00

$234.67

Which of these is the best estimate of his total earnings?

    A $400

    B $500

    C $600

    D $700

14 Which problem will have the greatest answer?

    F   45,769 – 997 = ___

    G   45,769 – 9.97 = ___

    H   45,769 – 0.997 = ___

    J   45,769 – 0.000997 = ___

15 Which symbol goes in the box below to give the smallest answer?

6 ☐ 2 =

A   +

B   −

C   ×

D   ÷

Sixteen people went to a pizza place and bought six pizzas. Each pizza had eight slices. Use this information to solve problems 16 and 17.

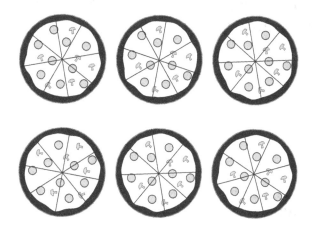

16 Which number sentence could be used to find the total number of slices purchased?

F   6 × 8 = ___

G   16 × 6 × 8 = ___

H   16 + 6 + 8 = ___

J   16 × 6 = ___

17 If everyone ate the same number of slices, how many did each person eat?

A   2

B   3

C   4

D   6

EAT YOUR VEGGIES

A class planted a vegetable garden as part of its science fair this year. Solve problems 18 through 21.

18 Hot peppers are planted in a part of the garden that is 6 feet across and 5 feet long. Each hot pepper plant requires a square area, 1 foot by 1 foot. How many pepper plants can be planted in this garden?

F   11

G   13

H   30

J   36

19 Helen's radish seeds sprouted after an even number of days. Which of these could not be the number of days it took for Helen's seeds to sprout?

A   3

B   4

C   6

D   10

20 Eggplant seeds sprouted in 14 days, lettuce seeds in 4 days, tomato seeds in 8 days, and bean seeds in 6 days. What is the correct order of seeds, from fastest sprouting to slowest sprouting?

F   eggplant, lettuce, tomato, bean

G   lettuce, bean, tomato, eggplant

H   eggplant, tomato, bean, lettuce

J   lettuce, tomato, bean, eggplant

21 Carrot seeds were planted on a Tuesday. They sprouted 10 days later. On which day of the week did the carrot seeds sprout?

A Monday

B Tuesday

C Thursday

D Friday

The graph below shows the heights of the tallest lettuce, pepper, tomato, and zucchini. Use the graph to solve problems 22 and 23.

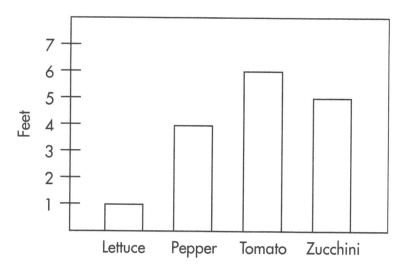

22 Which plant was the tallest of all?

F lettuce

G pepper

H tomato

J zucchini

23 How tall was the tallest pepper plant?

A 3 feet

B 4 feet

C 5 feet

D 6 feet

24 Which container holds the least milk?

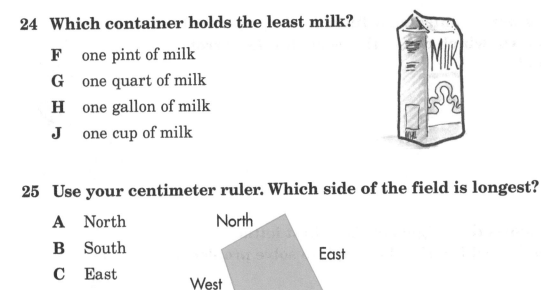

   F   one pint of milk

   G   one quart of milk

   H   one gallon of milk

   J   one cup of milk

25 Use your centimeter ruler. Which side of the field is longest?

   A   North

   B   South

   C   East

   D   West

North   East   West   South

26 Salerno's Bakery has its hours posted on a sign in its front window.

Salerno's

Hours
Monday—Friday
6AM—5PM

Weekends
7AM—7PM

How many hours is it open on Tuesday?

   F   9 hours

   G   11 hours

   H   12 hours

   J   13 hours

27 What is 4,569 rounded to the nearest 100?

   A   4,500

   B   4,570

   C   4,600

   D   5,000

28 What is another way to write the number thirty thousand, eight hundred four?

   F   30,804

   G   30,840

   H   3,840

   J   3,804

29 What number comes next in the pattern?

         2, 6, 10, 14, ?

   A   16

   B   18

   C   20

   D   140

30 Sally bought a number of 32-cent stamps using two $1 bills. Which of the following could be the change she got?

   F   4 cents

   G   6 cents

   H   8 cents

   J   10 cents

31 A 2-year-old boy is 30 inches tall. How many more inches must he grow before he is 4 feet tall?

   A   26 inches

   B   18 inches

   C   16 inches

   D   6 inches

32 Which figure has more than four sides?

   F   triangle

   G   square

   H   rectangle

   J   pentagon

Game Time

The picture below shows four different spinners that Belle, Kathy, James, and Paolo made to play a game. Look at the spinners. Then solve problems 33 through 35.

33 **Which student made the spinner with the greatest chance of landing on 2?**

A Belle

B Kathy

C James

D Paolo

34 **Which student made a spinner in which 1, 2, and 3 have equal chances?**

F Belle

G Kathy

H James

J Paolo

35 **Which student made the spinner in which 3 has a greater chance than 1?**

A Belle

B Kathy

C James

D Paolo

36 The figure shown is flipped across the line. What will the result look like?

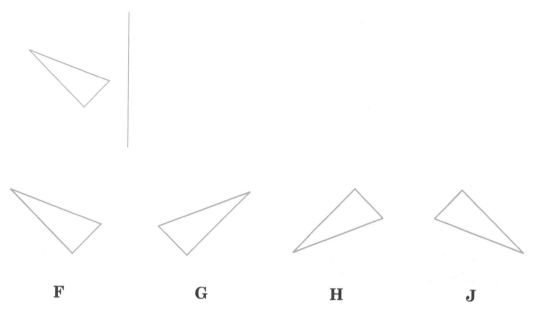

F   G   H   J

37 How many small cubes in all would you need to fill the cube shown?

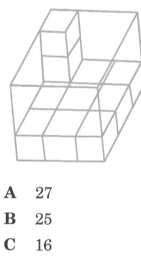

A   27

B   25

C   16

D   11

School Days

The Acadia School has grades 1 to 6. The table below shows the number of students in each grade. Study the table. Then use it to solve problems 38 through 40.

38 How many students are in grades 3 and 4 combined?

    F 232

    G 239

    H 242

    J 249

39 Which grade has the greatest number of students?

    A Grade 1

    B Grade 2

    C Grade 5

    D Grade 6

Grade	Number of Students
1	131
2	126
3	116
4	126
5	133
6	118

40 Which of the following can you not tell from the table?

    F the grade with the smallest number of students

    G the average number of students in a grade

    H the total number of students in the school

    J the number of teachers in the school

41 Which number sentence could be used to find the total number of party hats in the picture?

A $6 \times 6 \times 6 \times 6 =$ ___

B $5 \times 5 =$ ___

C $4 + 4 + 4 + 4 + 4 =$ ___

D $4 \times 6 =$ ___

42

Which figure is congruent to the figure above?

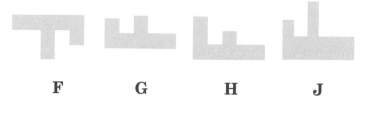

F   G   H   J

PATTERNS

Each of the squares in the figure below is numbered according to a pattern. Study the picture. Then use it to solve problems 43 and 44.

43 What number should be placed in the last entry of the third row?

A 1

B 2

C 3

D 4

44 If the table were completely filled in, how many times would the number 3 appear?

F 22

G 23

H 25

J 33

45 Which number sentence has an answer that is not a whole number?

A 148 + 32 = ___

B 148 − 32 = ___

C 148 × 32 = ___

D 148 ÷ 32 = ___

46 Which figure is $\frac{1}{4}$ shaded?

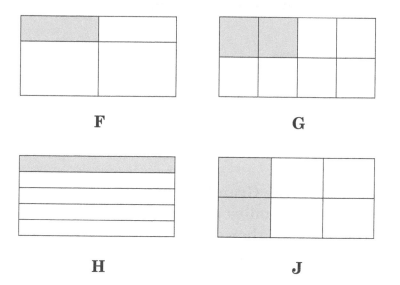

F

G

H

J

47 Two hundred fifty tourists will be traveling by bus to Washington, D.C. Each bus holds no more than 30 people. How many buses will be needed?

A 8

B 9

C 10

D 11

48 What number comes next in the pattern?

3, 5, 10, 12, 17, ___

F 25

G 22

H 19

J 18

49 Stephen asked Rebecca what her age was. She said, "Five years ago, I was three years older than you are now." Stephen is now nine years old. How old is Rebecca?

A   12

B   14

C   17

D   26

50 The Wu family traveled by car to visit the Grand Canyon. During the trip, their speed averaged 52 miles per hour. What else must you know to find how far they drove?

F   their average speed in each direction

G   how many days they spent on vacation

H   how many people are in the Wu family

J   the number of hours they drove

51 Ms. Young cut an apple pie into equal slices. Then she left to pick up her daughter at school. When she returned, she found that $\frac{1}{3}$ of the pie had been eaten by her sons. Use the picture below. How many slices did her sons eat?

A   5

B   4

C   3

D   2

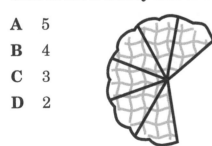

Use the map to solve problems 52 and 53.

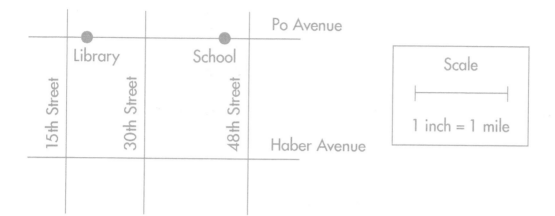

52 **Which of these roads are not parallel?**

   F   15th Street and 48th Street

   G   Po Avenue and Haber Avenue

   H   30th Street and Po Avenue

   J   15th Street and 30th Street

53 **Dulce walked from the school to the library and back. How far did she walk in all?**

   A   1 mile

   B   1.5 miles

   C   2 miles

   D   3 miles

54 **Louie's Ice Cream Shop sells vanilla, chocolate, and strawberry ice cream sodas. They come in small, medium, and large sizes. How many different ice cream sodas are there at Louie's?**

   F   9

   G   8

   H   7

   J   6

Weather Watching

During the 5 o'clock TV news, the weather reporter showed the table below. Use the table to solve problems 55 through 57.

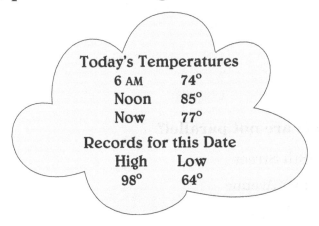

Today's Temperatures
6 AM   74°
Noon   85°
Now   77°
Records for this Date
High   Low
98°   64°

55 How did the temperature change today from 6 A.M. to noon?

   A   The temperature rose by 8 degrees.

   B   The temperature fell by 8 degrees.

   C   The temperature rose by 11 degrees.

   D   The temperature fell by 11 degrees.

56 Which number sentence could be used to find how much greater the record high is than the record low for this day?

   F $98 + 64 =$ ___

   G $98 - 64 =$ ___

   H $98 + 74 =$ ___

   J $98 - 74 =$ ___

57 What do you know after reading the table?

   A   It was cooler at 6 A.M. than at 5 P.M.

   B   The record temperatures for this date occurred one year apart.

   C   The temperature was higher during the news show than at noon.

   D   A new low record temperature will not be set today.

cm 1 2 3 4 5 6 7 8 9 10 11 12 13 14 15 16 17 18 19 20

1 2 3 4 5 6 7 8 inches

Answer Key

Reading

Lesson 1-pp. 7–13

S	D	leopards
1.	A	spying
2.	G	Howe told them where the Americans hid their guns.
3.	C	unseen
4.	H	tool
5.	D	the heat from the light bulb
6.	F	how to see the invisible writing
7.	B	fifty pounds
8.	J	no longer living
9.	B	They did not know that the sailors could hurt them.
10.	J	It could not fly.
11.	D	nesting
12.	H	There were too many things against the dodo birds.

Reading Review Test

Test-pp. 14–19

S	A	She sorts the clothes.
1.	C	using paint and colored paper to decorate the papier–mâché objects
2.	H	several days
3.	D	shirt
4.	H	what happens between a boy and his grandfather
5.	C	a special kind of Korean writing
6.	G	a ballpoint pen
7.	D	impressed
8.	G	"Wow," I said, holding the rice paper carefully.
9.	A	straighten
10.	F	its thinness

Language Arts

Lesson 2-pp. 20–21

SA	A	searched
SB	H	We bought ice cream cones and ate them on the way home.
1.	C	September 21, 2005
2.	F	Godfrey, Illinois
3.	C	he
4.	H	strongest
5.	C	You need milk or lemon juice.

Lesson 3-pp. 22–23

SA	B	I had a great time in Virginia.
SB	H	Get some dry dirt. We are going to make the dirt disappear.
1.	D	It is very important to be prepared.
2.	H	Ming takes very good care of her monkey.
3.	B	I like to read fairy tales more than anything else. They all have happy endings.
4.	F	The number of rings tells a tree's age.

Lesson 4-pp. 24–25

SA	C	The play lasted for over an hour.
SB	J	after sentence 4
1.	D	My parents told me that we were going on a trip to Disney World for spring vacation.
2.	H	I knew we were going to have a wonderful time.
3.	A	sentence 3

S	C	clapped
1.	B	When Joe Montana was in junior high school, he played football and basketball and ran track.
2.	J	After basketball practice, the school bus dropped him home at 5:30.
3.	A	So he missed the bus and had to find another way home.
4.	J	It is best as it is.
5.	C	His father called the school, and when they told him no one was there, he got worried.
6.	G	He came looking for Joe and, not finding him, called home.
7.	C	His parents wanted to know why Joe did not call them.
8.	F	Then he always had money to call them.
9.	B	sentence 2
10.	J	That is the best place to go see one.
11.	A	veterinarian
12.	J	healthy

Reading and Language Arts Comprehensive Test

Test-pp. 31–64

SA	C	have an enjoyable time
SB	F	The trunk works almost like a hand.
1.	C	small plant stems
2.	H	the last flower has grown
3.	C	when it's time to harvest the potatoes
4.	G	how to grow potatoes in a pot
5.	C	harvesting your crop
6.	G	helps the plant grow
7.	B	The shoots grow through the soil.
8.	J	kind
9.	A	We had turkey with stuffing and mashed potatoes.

10.	G	Be careful not to break the stems!
11.	B	The fence keeps animals out of the small yard.
12.	J	The fresh air makes me feel good. I love to watch my plants grow.
13.	A	in hollow trees
14.	G	thin flaps of skin
15.	A	climb
16.	J	a different kind of squirrel
17.	B	air currents
18.	H	a paper airplane
19.	B	glide
20.	H	swooped
21.	C	better
22.	G	excited
23.	D	rushed
24.	G	saving a whale
25.	A	He knew he could die.
26.	H	Yukio and the whale crying
27.	C	He will not stop throwing water on the whale until it is saved.
28.	J	his grandfather was too slow
29.	C	to keep him wet
30.	F	The tide came in and swept the whale free.
31.	B	huge, like a house
32.	H	He really cared about the whale.
33.	D	Yukio threw a pail of water on the whale stuck in the rocks.
34.	F	But usually we just fish off the dock.
35.	B	him
36.	H	December 19, 2005
37.	B	Portland, Oregon
38.	H	The whale breathes through its blowhole.
39.	D	active
40.	G	feels the music

41.	D	Box 4
42.	F	goes with her
43.	A	following quietly
44.	G	team
45.	A	games
46.	G	He had trouble writing.
47.	D	Nothing.
48.	H	He hoped Cal would find it easier to write his composition.
49.	C	Neither one was magic.
50.	G	come up with an idea for his composition
51.	D	his own imagination
52.	F	Believe in yourself and you can do it.
53.	C	The pencil from Angela worked better.
54.	J	in Part 5
55.	A	amazed
56.	H	It will help him arrange his thoughts.
57.	C	I could not sleep because it was the night before my trip.
58.	F	That is where the President lives.
59.	A	The sun shone brightly.
60.	J	It is best as it is.
61.	D	sentence 4
62.	H	My first stop was the Capitol Building.
63.	B	I was having so much fun, I did not want to go home.
64.	G	when George Lucas was a child
65.	C	by entertaining other children
66.	H	inventive
67.	B	Out of a cardboard box, George created a house with wallpaper on the walls and furniture in every room.
68.	F	the rides at an amusement park
69.	B	bored

70.	J	Follow your heart and you will succeed.
71.	D	a pioneer family
72.	F	The family made a house out of dirt.
73.	B	frightened
74.	J	enemies
75.	C	the wind made noise as it blew
76.	G	grateful
77.	C	Todd Reid is a 13-year-old tennis whiz.
78.	G	This company will also pay him to wear their clothing.
79.	A	Some people think that Todd is moving too fast.
80.	J	It is best as it is.

Mathematics

Lesson 1 - p. 67
S A
1. B
2. H

Lesson 2 - p. 68
S D
1. D
2. H

Lesson 3 - p. 69
S C
1. C
2. G

Lesson 4 - p. 70
S A
1. A
2. F

Lesson 5 - p. 71
S C
1. A
2. J

Lesson 6 - p. 72
S C
1. C
2. G

Lesson 7 - p. 73
S D
1. B
2. H

Lesson 8 - p. 74
S D
1. A
2. H

Lesson 9 - p. 75
S B
1. B
2. J

Mathematics Review Test

Test - pp. 76–80
S D
1. C
2. F
3. B
4. H
5. D
6. H
7. A
8. G
9. D
10. H
11. B
12. G
13. B
14. F
15. B
16. H
17. C

Mathematics Comprehensive Test

Test - pp. 81–82

SA   D

SB   G

SC   C

Part 1 - pp. 83–87

1. C
2. G
3. B
4. H
5. D
6. G
7. D
8. K
9. B
10. H
11. B
12. G
13. B
14. J
15. D
16. F
17. B

Part 2 - pp. 88–100

18. H
19. A
20. G
21. D
22. H
23. B
24. J
25. C
26. G
27. C
28. F
29. B
30. H
31. B
32. J
33. C
34. F
35. D
36. G
37. A
38. H
39. C
40. J
41. D
42. F
43. B
44. H
45. D
46. G
47. B
48. H
49. C
50. J
51. C
52. H
53. D
54. F
55. C
56. G
57. A

Reading and Language Arts Test Answer Sheet

STUDENT'S NAME

LAST — FIRST — MI

SCHOOL:
TEACHER:
FEMALE ○   MALE ○

CTB-TerraNova
Reading and Language Arts
Grade 4

BIRTH DATE

MONTH	DAY	YEAR
Jan ○	⓪ ⓪	⓪ ⓪
Feb ○	① ①	① ①
Mar ○	② ②	② ②
Apr ○	③ ③	③ ③
May ○	④	④ ④
Jun ○	⑤	⑤ ⑤
Jul ○	⑥	⑥ ⑥
Aug ○	⑦	⑦ ⑦
Sep ○	⑧	⑧ ⑧
Oct ○	⑨	⑨ ⑨
Nov ○		
Dec ○		

GRADE ③ ④ ⑤ ⑥ ⑦ ⑧

COMPREHENSIVE TEST: Reading and Language Arts

SA (A)(B)(C)(D)
SB (F)(G)(H)(J)

1 (A)(B)(C)(D)
2 (F)(G)(H)(J)
3 (A)(B)(C)(D)
4 (F)(G)(H)(J)
5 (A)(B)(C)(D)
6 (F)(G)(H)(J)
7 (A)(B)(C)(D)
8 (F)(G)(H)(J)
9 (A)(B)(C)(D)
10 (F)(G)(H)(J)
11 (A)(B)(C)(D)
12 (F)(G)(H)(J)
13 (A)(B)(C)(D)
14 (F)(G)(H)(J)
15 (A)(B)(C)(D)

16 (F)(G)(H)(J)
17 (A)(B)(C)(D)
18 (F)(G)(H)(J)
19 (A)(B)(C)(D)
20 (F)(G)(H)(J)
21 (A)(B)(C)(D)
22 (F)(G)(H)(J)
23 (A)(B)(C)(D)
24 (F)(G)(H)(J)
25 (A)(B)(C)(D)
26 (F)(G)(H)(J)
27 (A)(B)(C)(D)
28 (F)(G)(H)(J)
29 (A)(B)(C)(D)
30 (F)(G)(H)(J)
31 (A)(B)(C)(D)
32 (F)(G)(H)(J)

33 (A)(B)(C)(D)
34 (F)(G)(H)(J)
35 (A)(B)(C)(D)
36 (F)(G)(H)(J)
37 (A)(B)(C)(D)
38 (F)(G)(H)(J)
39 (A)(B)(C)(D)
40 (F)(G)(H)(J)
41 (A)(B)(C)(D)
42 (F)(G)(H)(J)
43 (A)(B)(C)(D)
44 (F)(G)(H)(J)
45 (A)(B)(C)(D)
46 (F)(G)(H)(J)
47 (A)(B)(C)(D)
48 (F)(G)(H)(J)
49 (A)(B)(C)(D)

50 (F)(G)(H)(J)
51 (A)(B)(C)(D)
52 (F)(G)(H)(J)
53 (A)(B)(C)(D)
54 (F)(G)(H)(J)
55 (A)(B)(C)(D)
56 (F)(G)(H)(J)
57 (A)(B)(C)(D)
58 (F)(G)(H)(J)
59 (A)(B)(C)(D)
60 (F)(G)(H)(J)
61 (A)(B)(C)(D)
62 (F)(G)(H)(J)
63 (A)(B)(C)(D)
64 (F)(G)(H)(J)
65 (A)(B)(C)(D)
66 (F)(G)(H)(J)

67 (A)(B)(C)(D)
68 (F)(G)(H)(J)
69 (A)(B)(C)(D)
70 (F)(G)(H)(J)
71 (A)(B)(C)(D)
72 (F)(G)(H)(J)
73 (A)(B)(C)(D)

74 (F)(G)(H)(J)
75 (A)(B)(C)(D)
76 (F)(G)(H)(J)
77 (A)(B)(C)(D)
78 (F)(G)(H)(J)
79 (A)(B)(C)(D)
80 (F)(G)(H)(J)

Mathematics Test Answer Sheet

STUDENT'S NAME		SCHOOL:
LAST	FIRST	MI	TEACHER:

SCHOOL:

TEACHER:

FEMALE ○   MALE ○

BIRTH DATE

MONTH	DAY	YEAR
Jan ○	⓪ ⓪	⓪ ⓪
Feb ○	① ①	① ①
Mar ○	② ②	② ②
Apr ○	③ ③	③ ③
May ○	④	④ ④
Jun ○	⑤	⑤ ⑤
Jul ○	⑥	⑥ ⑥
Aug ○	⑦	⑦ ⑦
Sep ○	⑧	⑧ ⑧
Oct ○	⑨	⑨ ⑨
Nov ○		
Dec ○		

GRADE ③ ④ ⑤ ⑥

CTB-TerraNova
Mathematics
Grade 4

COMPREHENSIVE TEST: Mathematics

SA Ⓐ Ⓑ Ⓒ Ⓓ Ⓔ
SB Ⓕ Ⓖ Ⓗ Ⓙ
SC Ⓐ Ⓑ Ⓒ Ⓓ

1 Ⓐ Ⓑ Ⓒ Ⓓ Ⓔ
2 Ⓕ Ⓖ Ⓗ Ⓙ Ⓚ
3 Ⓐ Ⓑ Ⓒ Ⓓ Ⓔ
4 Ⓕ Ⓖ Ⓗ Ⓙ Ⓚ
5 Ⓐ Ⓑ Ⓒ Ⓓ Ⓔ
6 Ⓕ Ⓖ Ⓗ Ⓙ Ⓚ
7 Ⓐ Ⓑ Ⓒ Ⓓ Ⓔ
8 Ⓕ Ⓖ Ⓗ Ⓙ Ⓚ
9 Ⓐ Ⓑ Ⓒ Ⓓ Ⓔ

10 Ⓕ Ⓖ Ⓗ Ⓙ
11 Ⓐ Ⓑ Ⓒ Ⓓ
12 Ⓕ Ⓖ Ⓗ Ⓙ
13 Ⓐ Ⓑ Ⓒ Ⓓ
14 Ⓕ Ⓖ Ⓗ Ⓙ
15 Ⓐ Ⓑ Ⓒ Ⓓ
16 Ⓕ Ⓖ Ⓗ Ⓙ
17 Ⓐ Ⓑ Ⓒ Ⓓ
18 Ⓕ Ⓖ Ⓗ Ⓙ
19 Ⓐ Ⓑ Ⓒ Ⓓ
20 Ⓕ Ⓖ Ⓗ Ⓙ
21 Ⓐ Ⓑ Ⓒ Ⓓ

22 Ⓕ Ⓖ Ⓗ Ⓙ
23 Ⓐ Ⓑ Ⓒ Ⓓ
24 Ⓕ Ⓖ Ⓗ Ⓙ
25 Ⓐ Ⓑ Ⓒ Ⓓ
26 Ⓕ Ⓖ Ⓗ Ⓙ
27 Ⓐ Ⓑ Ⓒ Ⓓ
28 Ⓕ Ⓖ Ⓗ Ⓙ
29 Ⓐ Ⓑ Ⓒ Ⓓ
30 Ⓕ Ⓖ Ⓗ Ⓙ
31 Ⓐ Ⓑ Ⓒ Ⓓ
32 Ⓕ Ⓖ Ⓗ Ⓙ
33 Ⓐ Ⓑ Ⓒ Ⓓ

34 Ⓕ Ⓖ Ⓗ Ⓙ
35 Ⓐ Ⓑ Ⓒ Ⓓ
36 Ⓕ Ⓖ Ⓗ Ⓙ
37 Ⓐ Ⓑ Ⓒ Ⓓ
38 Ⓕ Ⓖ Ⓗ Ⓙ
39 Ⓐ Ⓑ Ⓒ Ⓓ
40 Ⓕ Ⓖ Ⓗ Ⓙ
41 Ⓐ Ⓑ Ⓒ Ⓓ
42 Ⓕ Ⓖ Ⓗ Ⓙ
43 Ⓐ Ⓑ Ⓒ Ⓓ
44 Ⓕ Ⓖ Ⓗ Ⓙ
45 Ⓐ Ⓑ Ⓒ Ⓓ

46 Ⓕ Ⓖ Ⓗ Ⓙ
47 Ⓐ Ⓑ Ⓒ Ⓓ
48 Ⓕ Ⓖ Ⓗ Ⓙ
49 Ⓐ Ⓑ Ⓒ Ⓓ
50 Ⓕ Ⓖ Ⓗ Ⓙ
51 Ⓐ Ⓑ Ⓒ Ⓓ
52 Ⓕ Ⓖ Ⓗ Ⓙ
53 Ⓐ Ⓑ Ⓒ Ⓓ
54 Ⓕ Ⓖ Ⓗ Ⓙ
55 Ⓐ Ⓑ Ⓒ Ⓓ
56 Ⓕ Ⓖ Ⓗ Ⓙ
57 Ⓐ Ⓑ Ⓒ Ⓓ